Law and Politics in Peaceful Use of Nuclear Energy

Xinjun Zhang

Law and Politics in Peaceful Use of Nuclear Energy

知识产权出版社 有限责任公司
Intellectual Property Publishing House Co., Ltd.

Springer

Xinjun Zhang
School of Law
Tsinghua University
Beijing, China

ISBN 978-981-97-3815-1 ISBN 978-981-97-3813-7 (eBook)
https://doi.org/10.1007/978-981-97-3813-7

Jointly published with Intellectual Property Publishing House
The print edition is not for sale in China (Mainland). Customers from China (Mainland) please order the print book from: Intellectual Property Publishing House.
ISBN of the Co-Publisher's edition: 978-7-5130-6753-9

Translation from the Chinese language edition: "和平利用核能：核不扩散的法和政治" by Xinjun Zhang, © Intellectual Property Publishing House Co., Ltd. 2020. Published by Intellectual Property Publishing House Co., Ltd. All Rights Reserved.

This Springer imprint is published by the registered company Springer Nature Singapore Pte Ltd.
The registered company address is: 152 Beach Road, #21-01/04 Gateway East, Singapore 189721, Singapore

Preface

The general research interest of this study is in the role of a treaty deemed of highly political nature in a changing political environment. The study is designed to focus on the "inalienable right" to peaceful use of nuclear energy stipulated in Article IV of the Treaty on the Nonproliferation of Nuclear Weapons (NPT), and clearly not on the entirety of the NPT although it may involve contextual reading of other NPT articles. It is also not intended to appreciate or reject any particular interpretations established through employing the conventional "general rule of treaty interpretation" codified in the Vienna Convention on the Law of Treaties. Rather, this study questions the appropriateness of such an interpretive rule.

To this end, this study examines the evolution of rules and norms in the field of peaceful use of nuclear energy—it detects the source of dynamic obligations related to the peaceful use of nuclear energy and finds that the dynamic obligations outlined in the provisions of the NPT were intentionally made by states during treaty negotiation. The study further finds that subsequent international regulation of sensitive nuclear activities/technologies may be subjected to legal–illegal judgments by commentators based on their respective treaty interpretations. However, none of these perspectives are binding or necessarily compelling. Based on these findings, this study challenges the usefulness of the "general rule of interpretation" and proposes an interdisciplinary approach to interpretation for a better understanding of the role of dynamic treaty obligations within the nuclear nonproliferation regime.

Material in Chap. 3 was reproduced from "The Riddle of 'Inalienable Right' in Article IV of the Treaty on the Non-Proliferation of Nuclear Weapons: Intentional Ambiguity," *Chinese Journal of International Law* (2006), pp. 647–662. The author thanks Oxford University Press for permission to reproduce the copyrighted material. An excerpt of Chap. 5 as well as the bulk of Sects. 6.1–6.2 previously appeared in slightly different form as "Intentional Ambiguity and the Rule of Interpretation in Auto-interpretation: the case of 'inalienable right' in NPT Article IV," *Japanese Yearbook of International Law* (2009), pp. 35–66. The author thanks the International Law Association, Japan Branch, which holds the copyright for use on the internet.

An early version of Sects. 4.2–4.4 was presented at the International Conference on the Legal Issues of Peace Regime in the Korean Peninsula, held in Incheon, South Korea in December 2010.

Beijing, China Xinjun Zhang
zinjun@tsinghua.edu.cn

Contents

Chapter 1
"Inalienable Right" to Peaceful Use of Nuclear Energy and the Changing Nuclear Nonproliferation Regime

1.1 Introduction

No treaty has been as influential as the Treaty on the Nonproliferation of Nuclear Weapons (NPT).[1] However, this treaty has also provoked many controversies in contemporary international relations. No treaty is as favored by international relations (IR) scholars in their discussions on nuclear nonproliferation regimes[2] as the NPT;

[1] Treaty on the Nonproliferation of Nuclear Weapons, opened for signature July 1, 1968, entered into force March 5, 1970, extended indefinitely in the 1995 NPT Review and Extension Conference, 729 UNTS 161. Today, the NPT membership stands at 191 States. The Democratic People's Republic of Korea (DPRK) 2003 withdrawal is controversial but The UN Office for Disarmament Affairs maintains the DPRK on its listing of membership. (http://disarmament.un.org/treaties/t/npt).

[2] The NPT has already been widely accepted by international relations scholars as part of the international effort in preventing the proliferation of nuclear weapons. See Joseph S. Nye, *The International Nonproliferation Regime* (Stanley Foundation, 1980), p. 3; Joseph S. Nye, "Maintaining a Nonproliferation Regime," *International Organization*, Vol. 35 (1981), p. 16; Roger K. Smith, "Explaining the Non-proliferation Regime: Anomalies for Contemporary International Relations Theory," *International Organization*, Vol. 41 (1987), pp. 253–281; Benjamin N. Schiff, *International Nuclear Technology Transfer: Dilemmas of Dissemination and Control* (Rowman & Allanheld, 1984), pp. 22–29; Lawrence Scheinman, "Nuclear Safeguards and Non-proliferation in a Changing World Order," in William M Evan and Ved P. Nanda eds., *Nuclear Proliferation and the Legality ofNuclear Weapons* (University Press of America, 1995), p. 133; Peter Van Ham, *Managing Non-proliferation Regimes in the 1990: Power, Politics and Policies* (Royal Institute of International Affairs, 1994), pp. 38–40. On the relationship between the NPT and the nuclear nonproliferation regime, some commentators believe that the NPT is the central element of the regime. See Lawrence Scheinman, "Nuclear Safeguards and Non-proliferation in a Changing World Order," in William M Evan and Ved P. Nanda eds., *Nuclear Proliferation and the Legality of Nuclear Weapons* (University Press of America, 1995), pp. 133–134 (noting that the NPT is something in which the regime is "anchored."); Joseph S. Nye, "Maintaining a Nonproliferation Regime," *International Organization*, Vol. 35 (1981), p. 18; Joseph S. Nye, *The International Nonproliferation Regime* (Stanley Foundation, 1980), p. 7 (noting that the NPT has certainly become a central part of the regime); Roger K. Smith, "Explaining the Non-proliferation Regime: Anomalies for Contemporary International Relations Theory," *International Organization*, Vol. 41 (1987), p. 253, p. 257(noting that the NPT is more important than other instruments in the regime); Christer Ahlström, *The Status*

X. Zhang, *Law and Politics in Peaceful Use of Nuclear Energy*,
https://doi.org/10.1007/978-981-97-3813-7_1

however, controversies concerning the interpretation of certain NPT provisions have been largely overlooked as a subject of study by international lawyers.

One such controversy among nonproliferation scholars and practitioners is the interpretation of the "inalienable right" in the NPT Article IV. That provision reads as follows:

1. Nothing in this Treaty shall be interpreted as affecting the *inalienable right* of all the Parties to the Treaty to develop research, production and use of nuclear energy for peaceful purposes without discrimination and *in conformity with Articles I and II* of this Treaty.
2. All the Parties to the Treaty undertake to facilitate, and have the *right to participate* in, the fullest possible exchange of equipment, materials and scientific and technological information for the peaceful uses of nuclear energy. Parties to the Treaty in a position to do so shall also cooperate in contributing alone or together with other States or international organizations to the further development of the applications of nuclear energy for peaceful purposes, especially in the territories of non-nuclear-weapon States Party to the Treaty, with due consideration for the needs of the developing areas of the world.[3] (emphasis added).

What has made the issue of interpretation on the "inalienable right" more complicated is the divergent opinions on the phrase "in conformity with Articles I and II of this Treaty" in the same article. Articles I and II are as follows:

> Article I
>
> Each nuclear-weapon State Party to the Treaty undertakes not to transfer to any recipient whatsoever nuclear weapons or other nuclear explosive devices or control over such weapons or explosive devices directly, or indirectly; and not in any way to assist, encourage, or induce any non-nuclear-weapon State to *manufacture* or otherwise acquire nuclear weapons or other nuclear explosive devices, or control over such weapons or explosive devices.
>
> Article II
>
> Each non-nuclear-weapon State Party to the Treaty undertakes not to receive the transfer from any transferor whatsoever of nuclear weapons or other nuclear explosive devices or of control over such weapons or explosive devices directly, or indirectly; not to manufacture or otherwise acquire nuclear weapons or other nuclear explosive devices; and not to seek or receive any assistance in the *manufacture* of nuclear weapons or other nuclear explosive devices.[4] (emphasis added).

The confrontation between Iran and the United States on the Iranian uranium enrichment program illustrated profound disagreement.[5] While the "inalienable right" of the state parties to the NPT in the peaceful application of nuclear energy

---

of Multilateral Export Control Regimes: An Examination of Legal and Non-legal Agreements in International Co-operation (Iustus Förlag, 1999), p. 35 (noting that conventional obligations of the NPT "trigger" multilateral export control arrangements in the nuclear nonproliferation regime).

[3] Treaty on the Nonproliferation of Nuclear Weapons, 729 UNTS 161, *supra* note 1, art. IV.

[4] *Ibid.*, art. I and art. II.

[5] Peter Crail and James McMonigle, Stalemate in the Diplomatic Trenches: An Overview of the Diverging Positions at the 2005 NPT Review Conference, available at <http://cns.miis.edu/pubs/week/pdf/050516.pdf>.

has been "affirmed" on various occasions,[6] the scope of this right in the context of Articles I and II, where "manufacture" appears restricted, has never been clarified. This issue remains critical to international efforts to regulate sensitive nuclear activities/technologies as well as to exert more stringent international control over nuclear exports.

1.2 The Changing World: International Regulations on Sensitive Nuclear Activities/Technologies and Nuclear Exports

In response to India's nuclear explosion in 1974, the United States introduced multilateral and unilateral nuclear control measures in the mid-1970s. These actions marked the starting point of a new U.S. nonproliferation policy aimed at globally regulating sensitive nuclear activities. Sensitive nuclear activities cover technology, facilities, and materials related to uranium enrichment, plutonium reprocessing, and heavy water manufacturing that may directly contribute to the capacity of states to manufacture weapon-usable nuclear materials. These activities became designated as "sensitive" with the technical rationale stemming from their connection to immediate nuclear explosive capacity, rendering them proliferation-risky. Politically, controlling such activities, which had already been carried out in western non-nuclear-weapon states within civilian nuclear industry context, was also a sensitive matter.

For these countries, sensitive nuclear activities had been well incorporated into their domestic nuclear fuel cycles. Designating certain nuclear activities as inherently "sensitive" risked portraying them as intrinsically dangerous or malevolent. Because the new regulation on sensitive nuclear activities decoupled these nuclear activities from peaceful use of nuclear energy, it challenged the "inalienable right" (NPT Article IV) of all NPT States Party regarding the use of nuclear energy in sensitive fields.

The Ford and Carter Administrations carried out control measures through banning sensitive nuclear exports, intervening in recipient countries' indigenous fuel cycles, and interfering with other supplier states' sensitive nuclear exports. Immediate effects of the new U.S. nonproliferation policy fell upon the U.S. allies in Western

---

[6] The final documents of several NPT Review Conferences reiterated the affirmation. For example, the 1985 Final Decision on Article IV reads as follows, "...The Conference confirms that each country¡¯s choices and decisions in the field of peaceful uses of nuclear energy should be respected without jeopardizing their respective fuel-cycle policies…" See U.N. Doc. NPT/CONF.III/64/I (September 21, 1985). Similar wording can be found in the *1995 NPT Review and Extension Conference Decision 2*, U.N. Doc. NPT/CONF.1995/32 (Part I) (May 11, 1995), paras. 14-17; *The 2000 Final Document Vol. I*, U.N. Doc. NPT/CONF.2000/28 (Part I and II) (May 20, 2000), pp. 8–9; *Report of the Preparatory Committee on its Second Session*, U.N. Doc. NPT/CONF.2005/PC.II/50 (May 13, 2003), para. 41.

Europe and Japan, who had capacities for and interests in engaging in sensitive activities in their civilian nuclear industries. These countries opposed the introduction of the U.S. nonproliferation policy, claiming that it was not compatible with the NPT. To address such opposition, the United States for a time restrained from intervening in indigenous sensitive nuclear activities in these countries. In exchange, the advanced industrial countries agreed to coordinate their sensitive export policies within the U.S.-initiated framework of regulation (Nuclear Suppliers Group, NSG).

Currently, in addition to the NPT's categorization of haves (nuclear-weapon states) and have-nots (non-nuclear-weapon states), a new discriminatory structure appears to be emerging between Nuclear Supplier States (developed countries) and Nuclear Recipient States (developing countries). Advanced industrial countries with interest in and capacity to engage in sensitive nuclear activities may enjoy a broader "inalienable right," whereas developing countries of non-nuclear-weapon states are treated less preferentially regarding peaceful use of nuclear energy.

The situation appeared to deteriorate following the end of the Cold War. Supplier States expanded controls on nuclear activities from "sensitive nuclear activities" to dual-use items, as outlined in London Guideline Part Two. Moreover, Supplier States broadened the scope of controls to encompass "especially designed or prepared equipment and components" (EDP), which are essential in the peaceful use of nuclear energy, such as in nuclear power stations.[7] As a result of this policy change, Iran—an NPT member in good standing—faced trouble obtaining less proliferation-risky light water reactors from Russia.

1.3 The Controversy Over the Role of the NPT

The evolving regime of nuclear nonproliferation engendered many controversies among the NPT States Party following the treaty's entry into force in 1970. First, a question was asked about the lawfulness of indigenous sensitive nuclear programs, as seen during the trans-Pacific debate on the Japanese reprocessing program in the late 1970s. This raised whether sensitive nuclear activities should fall outside the scope of the "inalienable right" to peaceful nuclear energy use as defined in Article IV of the NPT. Second, a question arose concerning the lawfulness of industrialized nations exercising sensitive nuclear export control over developing countries. The answer to this question held potential implications for some European countries' nuclear exports policies and appeared as a trans-Atlantic dispute between the United States and some European countries in the second half of the 1970s, when Germany and France prepared sensitive exports to developing countries. Third, a question emerged around whether developing states have the right to engage in "sensitive nuclear activities," given the changing definition of such activities. This

[7] 1994 NSG "Non-Proliferation Principle" against countries with "proliferation concerns." See IAEA Document INFCIRC/539/Rev.1, p. 5.

appears particularly controversial from the perspective of a party state like Iran, which experiences difficulties engaging in conventional nuclear activities.

The NPT's "inalienable right" has proven an interpretive conundrum for nonproliferation scholars and practitioners regarding the evolving nuclear nonproliferation regime. The riddle involves three controversial interpretive issues. The first is the "inalienable right" itself. The second concerns the wording "in conformity with Articles I and II of this Treaty" and, consequently, the meaning of "manufacture" in Articles I and II. The third relates the nondiscrimination principle stipulated in Paragraph 2 of the NPT Article IV.[8]

In contrast with what had been advocated by the U.S.—that the NPT commitment not to "manufacture" nuclear weapons encompassed prohibitions on all related development, component fabrication, and testing—Japan and the European countries in the late 1970s insisted that the "inalienable right" faced no restrictions under the Treaty beyond the explicit ban on nuclear explosion. U.S. nonproliferation experts emphasized the wording "in conformity with Articles I and II of this Treaty" when interpreting "inalienable right." They interlinked the nonproliferation obligation in Articles I and II with "inalienable right." Joseph Nye, Deputy to the Under Secretary of State Security Assistance, Science and Technology and in charge of nonproliferation policies in the Carter Administration (January 1977–January 1979), wrote in 1980 justifying the U.S. new policy: "…a degree of restraint on sensitive exports at this time is not necessarily in conflict with Article IV or with the large bargain of the NPT. This conclusion is reinforced both by the language of the Article, which says it must be read in light of the obligation in Articles I and II."[9]

However, some scholars took the position that depriving sensitive nuclear activities from the "inalienable right" could not be assumed by interlinking Article IV to Articles I and II. For them, what mattered was whether Articles I and II could truly be interpreted as prohibiting sensitive nuclear activities. The early response of the United States toward European sensitive nuclear exports was marked as "spreading the bomb without quite breaking the rules."[10] Accordingly, sensitive nuclear exports do not necessarily fall within the scope of prohibition in Articles I and II. Such an interpretation would naturally lead to a broader scope of the permissive "inalienable right," notwithstanding the wording "in conformity with Article I and Article II."

The two entangled lines of argument relying on treaty interpretation indicate that the very nature of "inalienable right" was inherently ambiguous and contradictory, as some nonproliferation experts realized.[11] On one hand, the highly sensitive nature of security issues may have discouraged significant exploration of the "inalienable

---

[8] See "without discrimination" in Article IV(1) as well as the requirement of preferential treatment loosely defined as "due consideration for the needs of the developing areas" in Article IV(2).

[9] Joseph S. Nye, *The International Nonproliferation Regime*, *supra* note 2, p. 11.

[10] Albert Wohlstetter, "Spreading the Bomb Without Quite Breaking the Rules," *Foreign Policy*, Vol. 25 (1976–1977), pp. 152–154.

[11] Peter A. Clausen, "U.S. Nuclear Exports and the Nonproliferation Regime," in Jed C. Snyder and Samuel F. Wells, Jr. eds., *Limiting Nuclear Proliferation* (Ballinger Publishing Company 1985), p. 189. (In rejecting the view that cooperation in sensitive technologies should be excluded on the ground that it would constitute indirect assistance to the acquisition of nuclear explosives, Clausen

NPT achieved results in real-world politics. Indeed, in the study of nuclear nonproliferation, the NPT has already been widely accepted by nonproliferation experts—regardless of theoretical orientation—as part of international efforts to prevent the proliferation of nuclear weapons.[18] Some even assert it presents the central element of a nuclear nonproliferation regime "anchored" around the treaty.[19]

However, with a changing global landscape in the nuclear nonproliferation regime, issues of interpretation concerning the NPT have received less attention. Instead, some scholars and practitioners argue for formalizing arrangements to adapt the regime's underlying evolving political structure. People proposing this strain of regime theory thinking are labeled "Formalists," whose idea resembles positivist, rule-oriented legal perspectives. Formalists do not suspect the role of law in international relations but are more ready to suggest formal arrangements when existing law becomes incompatible with the underlying political transformations to sustain a positivist conception of the law.

The most straightforward approach involves treaty modification. Ryukichi Imai once suggested not to outlaw sensitive activities as a whole but to use a "more discriminatory approach." He proposed separating "unqualified states" from "qualified states" through treaty modification to resolve issues concerning the "inalienable right."[20] This modification, had it been realized, might have most accurately reflected the political reality in the nonproliferation regime.

Another Formalist consideration stems from the doctrine of *rebus sic stantibus*—the notion that a fundamental change in circumstances can be invoked as grounds for terminating a treaty.[21] For example, Joseph Pilat and Charle Nakhleh argued, "the NPT was based on certain assumptions about the availability and desirability of nuclear technologies. The ongoing debates about who should or should not supply what to whom show that these assumptions no longer hold true today."[22] However, the usefulness of the doctrine has always been a question mark for international lawyers. Hans Kelsen stated that "it is the function of law in general and treaties in particular to stabilize the legal relationship between states in the stream of changing circumstances... if circumstances did not change, the binding force conferred upon treaties by the law would be almost superfluous."[23] In the case of the NPT, although

[18] See *supra* note 2 and accompanying text.

[19] Ibid.

[20] Ryukichi Imai and Henry S. Rowen, *Nuclear Energy and Nuclear Proliferation: Japanese and American Views* (Westview Press, 1980), p. 45, p. 72, p. 167.

[21] Vienna Convention on the Law of Treaties, done at Vienna on May 23, 1969, entered into force on January 27, 1980, 1155 UNTS 331, art. 62.

[22] Joseph F. Pilat and Charles W. Nakhleh, "A Treaty Reborn? The NPT After Extension," in Raju G.C. Thomas ed., *The Nuclear Non-proliferation Regime: Prospects for the 21st Century* (St. Martin's Press, 1998), p. 48.

[23] Robert W. Tucker rev. and ed., Hans Kelsen, *Principles of International Law* (2nd ed. Holt, Rinehart & Winston, 1966), p. 359, p. 360 (noting that Kelsen also investigated literatures of international tribunal up to the year of 1952 and found no single case unreservedly confirmed the existence of this rule). See also Anthony Clark Arend, *Legal Rules and International Society* (Oxford University Press, 1999), p. 71.

rebus sic stantibus could theoretically justify announcing the demise of Article IV of the NPT, States Party have never invoked this rationale.

A third Formalist solution considers applying the rule of *lex posterior* to invalidate existing treaty obligations and rights. This approach assumes states may alter treaty rules through customary practice, first presuming a new customary international law emerges addressing the same subject matter. Through the *lex posterior* rule, the prior treaty rule is deprived of legal validity that it had provisionally achieved.[24] Some international lawyers have employed this approach. For example, regarding the U.N. Charter's Article 2(4) prohibition on the threat or use of force, Anthony Clark Arend and Robert Beck asserted states have effectively withdrawn their consent from the provision through customary practices and no longer truly accept the provision as law.[25]

By analogy, the "inalienable right" in Article IV of the NPT could potentially be seen as desuetude given emerging customary practices, as evidenced by states refraining from sensitive nuclear activities. However, this method has not featured in arguments about the legality of nuclear control practice in the application of the NPT. Two reasons may explain this. The first is the notorious difficulty in confirming the existence of an emerging customary rule. The second involves a problem in treaty–customary law relations: a new customary law does not inherently signify special intent to abrogate a prior incompatible treaty.[26]

Overall, the seeming erosion of the have-nots' right to peaceful use of nuclear energy in the evolving nonproliferation landscape creates many interpretive issues under the NPT, particularly the so-called "inalienable right" of non-nuclear-weapon states in Article IV. This study aims to explore this topic. As long as the NPT maintains legal force within the nuclear nonproliferation regime, the importance of this research is undoubtable. The research interest of the present author lies in treaty interpretation amid the changing political environment surrounding this highly politicized agreement. Specifically, an attempt is made to solve the riddle of the interpretation of "inalienable right" in Article IV of the NPT.

Dr. Mohamed ElBaradei, then Director General of the International Atomic Energy Agency (IAEA), sharply pointed out what lies behind the NPT logic in his address to the 2005 NPT Review Conference. "The Treaty has served us well for 35 years. But unless we regard it as part of a living, dynamic regime—capable of evolving to match changing realities, it will fade into irrelevance and leave us

[24] Ulrich Fastenrath, "Relative Normativity in International Law," *European Journal of International Law*, Vol. 4, No. 3 (1993), pp. 305-340.

[25] Anthony Clark Arend and Robert J. Beck, *International Law and the Use of Force: Beyond the U.N Charter Paradigm* (Routledge, 1993), p. 178.

[26] N. Kontou, *The Termination and Revision of Treaties in the Light of New Customary International Law* (Clarendon Press, 1994), p. 156. (According to Kontou, a new customary law, even having been confirmed in the practice, cannot automatically deprive the validity of a prior treaty rule. Kontou nevertheless suggests that a new customary law can be taken as a ground for treaty termination as well as modification, but various conditions are required when claimed so).

vulnerable and unprotected."[27] Dr. Mohamed ElBaradei's comment echoes research findings across international relations and international law on the dynamic nature of international norms, including treaty rules.

The present study examines the interplay of law and politics concerning the erosion of states' right to peaceful nuclear energy use as established under the NPT. Central to understanding the interplay is the concept of "dynamic treaty obligation." In a study on arms control agreements, Edwin Smith conceptualized "dynamic obligation" in international legal agreements:

> Dynamic international obligations result from agreements that are structured to allow consensual changes in the obligations imposed in order to fulfill the object of the treaty in uncertain conditions.[28]

"Dynamic obligation" indicates a treaty is not a finished product but undergoes continual construction through a consensual process. Thus, interpreting a treaty provision containing dynamic obligations requires understanding the "life cycle" [29] of that obligation: sources provide context for its development; "dynamic-ness" is made during negotiating and adopting the text of a specific treaty provision; and dynamic obligation lives on post-adoption as it adapts to changing circumstances.

This study comprehensively examines the evolution of the norm on the right to peaceful use of nuclear energy over time. Key questions include: what factors informed the potential design of dynamic treaty obligations; how were they incorporated into relevant treaty provisions; and how has subsequent practice impacted the interpretation or application of these dynamic obligations. By challenging the general rule of interpretation codified in the Vienna Convention on the Law of Treaties (VCLT), this research proposes an interdisciplinary perspective to better understand the role of the dynamic treaty obligation within the context of the nuclear nonproliferation regime—offering insight into both the legal and political dimensions of the issue.

---

[27] Statements of IAEA Director General Dr. Mohamed ElBaradei in the 2005 Review Conference of the Treaty on the Non-Proliferation of Nuclear Weapons, 2 May 2005, available at <https://www.iaea.org/newscenter/statements/treaty-non-proliferation-nuclear-weapons>.

[28] Edwin Smith, "Understanding Dynamic Obligations: Arms Control Agreements," *South California Law Review,* Vol. 64 (1990-1991), p. 1557. (Dynamic international obligations result from agreements that are structured to allow consensual changes in the obligations imposed in order to fulfill the object of the treaty in uncertain conditions).

[29] Martha Finnemore and Kathryn Sikkink, "International Norm Dynamics and Political Change," *International Organization* Vol. 52 (1998), p. 887. (noting that treaty is not a finished product but a matter under continual construction by consensual method. Therefore, "interpreting" a treaty requires an understanding of the "life cycle" of that treaty).

1.4 Outline of This Study

In Chap. 2, a pre-NPT historical survey is conducted that provides valuable insights into why states may have preferred dynamic obligations to be incoporated into the NPT framework. The analysis notes that in 1954, the U.S. nuclear control policy shifted from a strict technology denial policy to a liberal "Atoms for Peace" policy. The policy change demonstrated an inherent uncertainty in decision-making given insufficient knowledge of the consequence of the use of nuclear technology at the time. Such uncertainty necessitated periodic re-examination of national interests—interests which initially centered on strategic considerations alone but soon expanded to include potential economic gains from civilian nuclear trade.

Notwithstanding the U.S. nuclear nonproliferation policy in the pre-NPT era, whether and how to utilize nuclear energy remained squarely within sovereign states' purview. Other countries stakeholders in peaceful use of nuclear energy, such as Japan and West Germany, did not view their option of "going nuclear" as inherently inappropriate. A normative shift reframing appropriateness of going nuclear within a nonproliferation treaty risked undermining clarification efforts, particularly around parameters for peaceful use of nuclear energy. Both scientific and normative uncertainties constitute the source of dynamic obligations that were introduced into the NPT.

In Chap. 3, the focus is on how states incorporated dynamic obligations into the NPT's text, particularly through Article IV, which contains "inalienable right" and the "right to participate." However, properly contextualizing Article IV requires also examining Articles I and II, notebly the scope of "manufacture" barred under Article II. States' negotiating positions and deliberations on draft texts offered opportunities to clarify ambiguous provisions, but efforts for precision were countered by demands for ambiguity. Further analysis indicates ambiguity was motivated by needs for broad propaganda support and dominant states' individual control, and ambiguous language survived adoption despite some states seeking clarity—implying even they accepted necessary ambiguity.

Overall, the investigation into the *travaux préparatoires* of the NPT reveals how dynamic obligations were deliberately incorporated. The examination of *travaux préparatoires* indicates the dynamic nature of the NPT stems not from happenstance but intentional design during negotiations. Drafters purposefully imbued the agreement with dynamism to account for uncertainties in future state relations; they opted to allow the normative substance of provisions to be determined through the subsequent practice of states parties over time.

In Chap. 4, the relationship between the "inalienable right" and subsequent multilateral nuclear control measures is examined. Supplier states coordinated export control policies by concluding multilateral export control agreements. These agreements are not legally binding but constitute the unified and consistent practice of these states in applying the NPT. Since the United States first articulated its new nuclear nonproliferation policy on sensitive nuclear activities/technologies, these nuclear export control measures have expanded their scope from sensitive nuclear activities to dual-use and conventional nuclear (EDP) items.

This expansion of controls redrew the map of the nuclear nonproliferation world. The NPT's categorization of nuclear-weapon states versus non-nuclear-weapon states gave way to a new division of regulating states (Nuclear Supplier States, developed countries) and regulated states (Nuclear Recipient States, developing countries). Within the NPT framework, a novel "haves" and "have-nots" dynamic evolved with developed non-nuclear-weapon states enjoying broader "inalienable right" versus developing counterparts facing more restrictions. This regulating–regulated structure risks conflict between supplier and recipient states regarding compatibility with Article IV's enshrinement of all states' "inalienable right" to peaceful nuclear energy—an issue that centres on treaty interpretation.

However, the very nature of dynamic obligations does not lend themselves to a legal–illegal judgment based solely on a textual–contextual interpretation of the relevant NPT provisions. Indeed, developing Party States did retain opportunities for clarification and conclusion regarding the scope of their treaty rights through the NPT Review Conferences, even if a formal judicial ruling was unavailable. The 1995 NPT Review and Extension Conference presented the greatest such chance, as states decided there whether to extend the Treaty—giving developing countries unprecedented bargaining leverage they previously lacked. However, with respect to the Review and Extension Conference, developing countries of the NPT parties failed to leverage this opportunity effectively; the decisions concluded at the Conference helped little in clarifying the scope of the right to nuclear energy under the NPT Article IV. Rather, the dynamic obligations of relevant NPT provisions suggest that multilateral nuclear controls may potentially provide an "authentic interpretation" of the "inalienable right." Nevertheless, achieving "the agreement of the parties regarding its interpretation" remains elusive due to the entrenched, discriminatory nature of the regulating—regulated structure.

In Chap. 5, the analysis hones in on the interpretive challenge concerning states' "inalienable right." In the absence of a competent institutional organ that is capable of rendering authoritative interpretations binding on all states, decentralized legal system initially and equally entrusts autointerpretation to each state to settle the conflicts between norms and their interpretation. When assessing such autointerpretations, the "general rule of interpretation" codified in Article 31 and the "supplementary means of interpretation" in Article 32 of the Vienna Convention on the Law of Treaties seem most relevant legal criteria, as states are bound by the said rules in making autointerpretations.

This chapter provides necessary context on the issue of interpretation under Article IV of the NPT by briefly reviewing the arguments surrounding events triggered by shifts in the U.S. policy controlling sensitive nuclear activities. This background indicates that the "inalienable right" rather than the "right to participate," poses the true interpretive conundrum due to its ambiguous scope of conferred rights and obligations. This chapter then examines various autointerpretations concerning the "inalienable right" primarily relying on the general interpretive rule under the VCLT Article 31, especially in the context of the North Korean and Iranian nuclear crises.

However, Article 31 provides little clarification for the ambiguous "inalienable right" in Article IV of the NPT. While a restrictive reading may be supported by the textual approach, a teleological approach leads to the opposite conclusion, and subsequent practice yielded only ambiguity and confusion. Completely different conclusions on the interpretation of the "inalienable right" appear drawable based primarily on Article 31, highlighting its limited utility in this context.

In Chap. 6, an interdisciplinary perspective is proposed to better comprehend the interpretive riddle surrounding the "inalienable right" to peaceful use of nuclear energy in the changing world of nuclear nonproliferation. Constructivist theory is critically applied to challenge the traditional textual–contextual rule of treaty interpretation. Key Constructivism's concepts help elucidate the dynamic nature of treaty rules and their interpretation. At the ontological level, Constructivists views treaties not as static with regulative functions only, but as social structures evolving through agent-structure interaction and continuous intersubjective construction. Methodologically, Constructivists criticize the inductive derivation of the general interpretive rule (VCLT Article 31) from limited pre-1969 case samples of international and domestic judicial decisions. They reject such an inductive method because the "samples" were limited to available court rulings. However, as international courts and tribunals lack compulsory jurisdiction, they cannot adjudicate cases involving interpretations of treaties in sensitive security and other issue areas states are reluctant to submit.

In Chap. 7, the central argument is presented to resolve the riddle of treaty interpretation. It is posited that subsequent practice should not become a target of legal–illegal judgment under static, regulative treaty rules but rather be viewed as an integrated part of a dynamic obligation process. Subsequent practice can be understood through the lens of "treaty interpretation by subsequent practice" under the VCLT Article 31(3)(b). However, the nature of "dynamic obligation" implies subsequent practice should hold equal norm-creating effect to interpretation. Study on *travaux préparatoires* of the 1969 Vienna Convention on the Law of Treaties and the international judicial practice confirms treaty modification and interpretation intertwine closely. Moreover, determining the relevant subsequent practices to ascertain "agreement of the Parties regarding its interpretation" per Article 31(3)(b) proves difficult, underscoring the need for theoretical insights on the "source" of international law.

A central claim in international law-making posits that in addition to state consents, constitutive or extraneous rules must complement consents to enable norm creation. This opens possibilities for creating dynamic obligations. *Pacta sunt servanda*, a norm that cannot derive directly from consent, has long been viewed as a default constitutive rule for treaties. While traditional consent doctrine views *pacta sunt servanda* as a rule validating static, regulative treaty rules, other legal theories propose alternative validating extraneous rules—from Hart's secondary rule and Frank's concept of legitimacy to the "human indignity" of the New Haven School and the recent revival of Fuller's theory of "internal morality." None necessarily conclude obligations must remain static; each reflects Constructivist influence to varying degrees in accounting for dynamic norm-building processes beyond consent alone.

In this analysis, Fuller's concept of "internal immorality" appears promising for establishing "agreement of the Parties regarding its interpretation" given its understanding of legal norms as rooted in pervasive interaction of ends and means. Fuller emphasizes the mutuality of governors and the governed, precluding social control solely through rules. Efforts to improve transparency in export controls and establish frameworks for dialog and cooperation among all interested NPT states point to potential ways to help bridge regulatory divides in ongoing, good-faith interpretation processes concerning states' "inalienable right" to peaceful use of nuclear energy. This may prove a more constructive approach respecting the dynamic, socially constructed nature of treaty norms.

Chapter 2
Historical Survey of the Pre-NPT Nuclear Nonproliferation Regime: The Emergence of Dynamic Obligations

2.1 Introduction

This chapter analyzes the evolution of the nuclear nonproliferation regime prior to the conclusion of the NPT. The survey aims to provide a better understanding of the formation of dynamic obligations—the factors rendering the NPT commitments flexible over time. I will introduce an intermediary concept of uncertainty between examining pretreaty development and how treaties construct dynamic obligations, arguing uncertainty primarily causes their emergence. To this end, pretreaty state practices are referenced to explore sources of uncertainty.

Pretreaty history study relevance to treaty interpretation in areas enabling dynamic obligation has been largely overlooked. Treaty interpretation commonly presumes provisions have a single determinable meaning, as codified in the 1969 Vienna Convention on the Law of Treaties. However, research in international relations suggests this view may be too narrow when examining real-world dynamics—states also agree to ambiguous wording intentionally leaving meaning open to ongoing interpretation. Accounting for this provides a more nuanced understanding of how treaties function in practice.

This chapter is divided into two parts. The first examines the explanatory framework for factors leading to the creation of dynamic obligations. The "institutional design" mechanism illustrating dynamic obligations provides initial indicators—I argue that uncertainty is critical in creating dynamic obligations in the security domain. Research on "institutional design" also categorizes the factors that contribute to uncertainty, useful for comprehending the formation of dynamic obligations.

The second part is empirical. Following the established explanatory framework, it examines the pre-NPT nuclear nonproliferation regime's evolution and investigates whether the factors comprising uncertainty can be identified in pre-negotiation state practice. Special attention is paid to certain nuclear activities justifiable for peaceful purposes yet highly proliferation-risky. An unsettling change in national interests is observed regarding these as security concerns and economic interests came

X. Zhang, *Law and Politics in Peaceful Use of Nuclear Energy*,
https://doi.org/10.1007/978-981-97-3813-7_2

into conflict. Uncertainty increases with the development of nuclear technology potentially rendering some nuclear activities more proliferation-risky.

2.2 The Sources of Dynamic Obligation: An Explanatory Framework

In a study on arms control agreements, Edwin Smith conceptualized "dynamic obligation" in international legal agreements, noting:

> Dynamic international obligations result from agreements that are structured to allow consensual changes in the obligations imposed in order to fulfill the object of the treaty in uncertain conditions.[1]

Edwin Smith further noted four potential uncertainty sources: (1) States may acknowledge changing economic relations or technological capacities could create future risk. (2) Important facts affecting cooperation gains may be uncertain. (3) Precise risk levels may be unknown. (4) States may not be certain about the proper response strategy to an admittedly serious risk.[2] He derived this from observing certain arms control agreements.

While Smith's observation provides valuable insights, it alone may not suffice to establish an explanatory framework. Institutional design proved instructive, as its generic dynamic obligation concept examines sources more comprehensively. Researchers of institutional design similarly focus on uncertainty alongside other factors in illuminating flexible commitments over time. In reviewing institutional design studies, factors leading to dynamic obligations treated insufficiently by Smith can be discussed further.

2.2.1 *Uncertainty*

The "logic of expected consequences" presumes states know their interests when developing an institution. Ideally, states would know each consequence and precisely calculate behaviors to further interests. However, in reality, states lack omniscience and cannot anticipate every consequence of an event. Therefore, uncertainty is raised as a factor necessitating the ideal model's modification to account for limitations on rational instrumental action.[3]

---

[1] Edwin Smith, "Understanding Dynamic Obligations: Arms Control Agreements," *South California Law Review*, Vol. 64 (1990–1991), p. 1557.

[2] *Ibid.*, pp. 1557–1558.

[3] Alexander Wendt, "Driving with the Rearview Mirror: On the Rational Science of Institutional Design," *International Organization*, Vol. 55 (2001), p. 1029. Theories of bounded rationality and ambiguity have resulted in significant modifications in the classical theory of rational instrumental action. However, like the theories they criticize, they largely assume a logic of consequences. See

Uncertainty challenges assumptions that states can apprehend stable, exogenous national interests. It questions the static nature of international norms and rules when made through consent under such an assumption. Koremenos, Lipson, and Snidal, in introducing the "Rational Design project," proposed flexibility increases institutionally in response to worldly uncertainty.[4] This conjecture finds strong support in case studies within the project.[5]

Koremenos, Lipson, and Snidal note uncertainty over state participation in world affairs should consider states' knowledge regarding consequences of their own actions, other's actions, and the actions of international institutions. Relevant knowledge encompasses scientific/technical and political/economic types.[6] "Flexibility" is described roughly as an institutional design accommodating new environmental realities.[7]

Some argued notions of uncertainty and flexibility were too abstract for empirical verification.[8] One problem noted was the Rational Design project did not distinguish risk from uncertainty, an important delineation in rational choice economics. In reviewing the project, Wendt saw this distinction as key to designing flexibility effectively.[9] "Risk" refers to unknown outcomes within known possibilities, involving incomplete information.[10] Under this type of uncertainty, agreeing flexiblity is rational for states.[11]

Wendt noted uncertainty's complexity challenges Rational Design's usefulness. He identified "genuine uncertainty,"[12] where states lack competence to comprehend true problems—probabilities themselves are indeterminable.[13] Under such uncertainty, Wendt suggested states follow simple, rigid rules rationally. In the

James G. March and Johan P. Olsen, "The institutional dynamics of international political orders," *International Organization*, Vol. 52 (1998), p. 950.

4 Barbara Koremenos, Charles Lipson, and Duncan Snidal, "The Rational Design of International Institutions," *International Organization*, Vol. 55 (2001), p. 793.

5 Barbara Koremenos, Charles Lipson, and Duncan Snidal, "Rational Design: Looking Back to Move Forward," *International Organization*, Vol. 55 (2001), pp. 1055–1056.

6 Barbara Koremenos, Charles Lipson, and Duncan Snidal, *supra* note 4, p. 778.

7 *Ibid.*, p. 773.

8 John Duffield, "The Limits of 'Rational Design'," *International Organization*, Vol. 57 (2003), pp. 425–426. The authors of Rational Design Project admitted that the concept of flexibility needed to be refined. See Barbara Koremenos and Duncan Snidal, "Moving Forward, One Step at a Time," *International Organization*, Vol. 57 (2003), p. 435.

9 Alexander Wendt, *supra* note 3, pp. 1029–1031.

10 *Ibid.*, p. 1030.

11 *Ibid.*, p. 1031.

12 This term is from Ronald Heiner. He proposed that genuine uncertainty resulted from a gap in an agent's decision competence relative to the difficulty in selecting more preferred alternatives. See Ronald Heiner, "The Origin of Predictable Behavior," *The American Economic Review*, Vol. 73 (1983), p. 571.

13 Alexander Wendt, *supra* note 3, p. 1031.

context of institutional design, rational action entails minimizing rather than maximizing flexibility and individual control.[14]

Wendt acknowledged lacking empirical evidence for "genuine uncertainty" speculations.[15] Thus he restricted conjectures to areas like human rights, where "logic of appropriateness" dominates.[16] However, justifying such restriction or empirically supporting this research path was not provided. Speculating on "genuine uncertainty" seems to *prima facie* contradict the result of case studies made in the Rational Design project, as Koremenos, Lipson and Snidal found human rights agreements more likely to incorporate escape clauses[17] (promoting flexibility and individual control). "Genuine uncertainty" appears providing theoretical variety but less empirical utility at this time.

Indeed, economic analysis on "genuine uncertainty" originated observing nonhuman behavior,[18] where knowledge attribution proves difficult. However, international relations involve sophisticated bureaucratic decision-making as actors seek information to reduce competence gaps versus problem difficulty.[19] For such decision makers, the challenge appears as a matter of more or less knowledge, or weaker or greater uncertainty rather than an absolute dichotomy. Further empirical examination of uncertainty types in practice could strengthen theoretical framing.

Notably, in a soft law study co-authored with Kenneth W. Abbott, Snidal himself followed the risk-uncertainty distinction and asserted its significance regarding precision,[20] an index of flexibility. This research suggests precise agreements manage risk but under fundamental uncertainty, states prefer imprecision to avoid unfavorable commitments. This did not contradict the Rational Design conjectures, as index of flexibility[21] could offset via blending.[22] Abbott and Snidal imply challenges exist in selecting flexibility indexes. Overall, their analysis found states tend toward imprecise provisions when uncertainty increases.

---

[14] *Ibid.*, p. 1031.

[15] *Ibid.*, p. 1030.

[16] *Ibid.*, p. 1032.

[17] See Barbara Koremenos, Charles Lipson, and Duncan Snidal, *supra* note 5, p. 1062, at note 15.

[18] Ronald Heiner, *supra* note 12, p. 562.

[19] This is Heiner's conceptualization about uncertainty (the C-D gap). See *Ibid.*

[20] Kenneth W. Abbott and Duncan Snidal, "Hard and Soft Law in International Governance," *International Organization*, Vol.54 (2000), p. 442.

[21] Barbara Koremenos, Charles Lipson, and Duncan Snidal, *supra* note 4, pp. 793–794 (containing imprecision clauses, evading clauses, reviewing clauses as well as withdrawing clauses).

[22] Kenneth W. Abbott and Duncan Snidal, *supra* note 20, p. 442, at note 56 (incorporating reviewing conference into flexibility in case of precise agreement).

2.2.2 *The Forms of Dynamic Obligations and the Utility in the Security Issue Area*

Abbot and Snidal provide an important clue for interdisciplinary research on dynamic obligations—that flexibility is selective. They suggest it can be maintained through arrangements such as escape clauses, withdrawing clauses, reviewing clauses, and clauses that permit renegotiation. However, compared to periodically adopting *ad hoc* arrangements, "imprecision" or "ambiguity" in specific wording is an inherent, low-effort design for flexibility.

Dynamic obligations need not preclude *ad hoc* arrangements like reviewing or withdrawing clauses. Reviewing clauses maintain consensual change, whereas withdrawing clauses allow states no longer tolerating flexible changes. However, ambiguity coexists less readily with escape clauses requiring precision defining the "escaped" rule.[23] Among the flexibility devices, imprecise rulemaking appears the lowest-effort option versus escape clauses necessitating negotiated precision.[24] Reviewing and withdrawing clauses also invoke higher costs than escape clauses when enacted. Together, this implies ambiguity comprises a primary flexibility-enabling mechanism.[25]

In security domains featuring fluid state relations and rapid technological change, decision-making complexity intensifies as uncertainty becomes more fundamental. States also prioritize secrecy regarding security information. Under such circumstances, dynamic obligations negotiated via ambiguous provisions comprise not only a low-effort flexibility mechanism, but a means for states to avoid legal-illegal judgments that could catalyze sanctions or military escalations. Even the risk of ineffective sanctions reinforces incentives for adopting ambiguity and embedded dynamic obligations when drafting security treaties.

2.2.3 *Normative Factors in Designing Dynamic Obligations*

However, the Rational Design project gave little consideration to normative factors impacting institutional design. Wendt alternatively suggested explaining design by incorporating the "logic of appropriateness"—that states consent to arrangements they perceive as normatively appropriate, not solely based on rational self-interest calculations.[26]

---

[23] Judith Goldstein and Lisa L. Martin, "Legalization, Trade Liberalization, and Domestic Politics: A Cautionary Note," *International Organization*, Vol. 54 (2000), pp. 623–626.

[24] For example, the GATT/WTO safeguard mechanisms aim to protect states from import pressures. However, invoking the escape clause can be costly as it may provoke retaliation from states against which that escape clause has been applied. See GATT Article 19(3) a.

[25] Peter B. Rosendorff and Helen Milner, "The Optimal Design of International Trade Institutions: Uncertainty and Escape," *International Organization*, Vol. 55 (2001), p. 831.

[26] Alexander Wendt, *supra* note 3, p. 1021.

One challenge regarding the "logic of appropriateness" is its subjective nature, as appropriateness judgments can vary widely. Additionally, incorporating this concept may not yield definitive empirical results.[27] Normative and ideational factors prove difficult to measure objectively and are often methodologically sidelined for this reason.[28]

As "appropriateness" standards stem from prior norms, challenging an existing logic of appropriateness requires demostrating explicit "inappropriateness."[29] Legal study provides one approach, as precedence guides legal arguments and new institutions must fit existing frameworks.[30] In this view, "appropriateness" largely results from legal analogy and contingency over time.

However, the picture is mixed. Positivist international lawyers seem to have overemphasized voluntarism, refusing normative factors in the treaty-making process. For example, Prosper Weil saw that law was within the confinement of "voluntarism." For him, even *jus cogens* and *erga omnes* norms were not considered in the context of "voluntarism" because these two norms challenged a "pluralistic, heterogeneous" international system.[31] Meanwhile, recent studies demonstrate normative elements impacting decision-making. For example, Nina Tannenwald's study showed belief facilitated the nuclear taboo.[32] Klotz suggested global norms facilitated domestic acceptance of anti-apartheid norms. Alternatively, reconstructed national interests strengthened global norms.[33] Finnemore and Sikkink argued that domestic influences strongly shape emerging international norms.[34]

Ultimately, normative factors may also enable dynamic obligations. One view is that dynamic obligations more readily emerge regarding pending treaty norms lacking contemporaneous social context appropriateness. Abrupt shifts in appropriateness allow a "grace period" for embracing changed norms as inconsistent state practice continues. Dynamic obligations help adjust to managing new appropriateness standards. Consequently, treaty obligations gain "dynamism" facilitating normative adjustment. For example, diffuse bigamous cultural practices informed ambiguous human rights language.[35] Diffusion potentially stemmed from strategic or economic reasons. This point is further illustrated in the survey of pre–NPT history.

---

[27] Wendt attempted to introduce the "logic of appropriateness" into genuine uncertainty. However, the theoretical analysis and empirical application of this concept appear somewhat underdeveloped.

[28] Martha Finnemore and Kathryn Sikkink, "International Norm Dynamics and Political Change," *International Organization*, Vol. 52 (1998), p. 889.

[29] *Ibid.*, p. 897.

[30] *Ibid.*, p. 915.

[31] Prosper Weil, "Towards Relative Normativity in International Law?" *American Journal of International Law*, Vol. 77 (1983), p. 420.

[32] Nina Tannenwald, "The Nuclear Taboo: The United States and the Normative Basis of Nuclear Non-Use," *International Organization*, Vol. 53 (1999), pp. 433–468.

[33] Audie Klotz, "Norms Reconstituting Interests: Global Racial Equality and U.S. Sanctions against South Africa," *International Organization*, Vol. 49 (1995), pp. 451–478.

[34] Martha Finnemore and Kathryn Sikkink, *supra* note 28, pp. 886–899.

[35] Convention on the Elimination of All Forms of Discrimination against Women, opened for signature Dec. 18, 1979, entered into force Sept. 3, 1981, 1249 U.N.T.S. 13, art. 16.

2.3 The Emergence of Dynamic Obligations in the Pre-NPT Nuclear Nonproliferation Regime

In this section, the evolution of the nuclear nonproliferation regime prior to the NPT will be surveyed. The purpose is to understand uncertainties and normative factors presented in the pre-NPT era, and explain what led states to opt for dynamic obligations incorporated into NPT provisions.

Technological uncertainty due to limited nuclear knowledge initially prompted strict U.S. control policy. However, shifting national interests toward civilian nuclear trade's economic potential facilitated a transition to a flexible, liberal "Atoms for Peace" approach. National interests broadened beyond exclusive security concerns. Particular attention involved "sensitive activities" relating to the manufacture of plutonium and uranium. Discriminating control of sensitive exports necessitated policy nuance and flexibility.

2.3.1 Strict Technology Denial: "Genuine Uncertainty"?

The notion of "genuine uncertainty" necessitating rigid rules appears exemplified by the United States' strict technology denial policy prior to 1954. This involved a comprehensive ban on disseminating nuclear technology to any countries, suggesting an attempt to impose rigid control in an environment of significant uncertainty regarding proliferation dynamics.

However, some international cooperation existed between the United States and its close allies. During wartime, the United Kingdom and Canada cooperated in the U.S.-led nuclear weapons project. The 1943 Quebec agreement determined they would not spread any information to third parties without mutual consent[36] and agreed to a monopoly of uranium against third parties.[37] This wartime Anglo-Saxon arrangement was confirmed post-Hiroshima in 1945.[38] While facilitating nuclear cooperation, the U.S. policy of technology denial still restricted Anglo-Canadian access to sensitive fields during joint research.[39] Wartime cooperation ultimately ended under the 1946 U.S. McMahon Act' stringent domestic and foreign control of all nuclear weapons knowledge and materials.[40]

---

[36] Bertrand Goldschmidt, "A Historical Survey of Nonproliferation Policies," *International Security*, Vol. 2 (1977), p. 70.

[37] W. K. Domke, "Proliferation, Threat, and Learning: The International and Domestic Structures of Export," in Marianne van Leeuwen ed., *The Future of the International Nuclear Non-proliferation Regime* (M. Nijhoff Publishers, 1995), pp. 207–208.

[38] *Ibid.*, p. 208. See also Bertrand Goldschmidt, *supra* note 36, p. 70.

[39] *Ibid.*, p. 208.

[40] Atomic Energy Act of 1946, Pub. L. No. 79–585, 60 Stat. 755, 755–75 (codified as amended at 42 U.S.C. §§ 1801–1819).

Under the "genuine uncertainty" logic, the strict technology denial policy represented a rational response given complete lack of knowledge distinguishing civilian and military use of nuclear energy. However, this "genuine uncertainty" becomes untenable more readily as knowledge diffuses—as exemplified by emerging civilian nuclear reactor technology.

The U.S. Navy's nuclear submarine program informed civilian light water reactor development into pressurized water reactors and boiling water reactors. Two features conferred proliferation resistance: using only low-enriched uranium (less than 3% of uranium 235) which cannot be used directly for weapons without further enrichment strictly controlled by the U.S.; and generating unsuitable plutonium in spent fuel for bombs.[41] Under continued controls over enrichment technology and natural uranium, light water reactors thus mitigated proliferation risks from both uranium and plutonium pathways. This technical evolution was integral to shifting nonproliferation approaches.

An alternative to light water reactors was the heavy water reactor developed in the 1950s by Canada, the United Kingdom, and France. From a nonproliferation perspective, heavy water reactors' continuous fuel unloading capability facilitated easier plutonium production for nuclear explosions. India's 1974 nuclear test device allegedly utilized supplied Canadian heavy water reactor technology.

As a result, calls grew to reform the rigid technology denial policy. The emergence of civilian nuclear power stations demonstrated peaceful nuclear applications and proliferation-resistant technological options, thereby reducing "genuine uncertainty." As understanding developed, the rationale upholding the rigid technology denial policy diminished. This progression understandably gave rise to calls to reform inflexible nonproliferation approaches and instead permit cooperation leveraging growing nuclear expertise. Technological advancement thus informed evolving perspectives on necessary and prudent controls.

Other factors also prompted discarding of policy rigidity. Effectiveness concerns arose regarding strict technology denial policy. For example, denying Canadians plutonium access during wartime cooperation reportedly spurred independent research yielding a new plutonium extraction method (the solvent extraction method) with French cooperation.[42] Additionally, the Soviet Union tested an atomic weapon in 1949 and the UK in 1952, further evidencing technology denial's limited effectiveness.

---

[41] Among plutonium isotopes, pure plutonium-239 is suitable for plutonium-type nuclear weapons. When mixed with other isotopes like plutonium-240, it results in lower yields and greater uncertainty in detonation. In the case of light water reactor, the normal production process keeps the fuel remaining long time in the reactor and thus produces a large fraction of plutonium-240 in spent fuel. If one wants to keep the fraction of plutonium-240 low in the spent fuel produced by the water light reactor, an abnormal course can be designed by discharging the irradiated fuel long before it has been fully utilized. Nevertheless, this abnormal course will increase supply of low-enriched uranium, which in turn is costly and easy to be detected by supplier states as far as supplier states monopoly uranium enrichment and retain the leverage of supplying low-enriched uranium. See Carl Walske, "Nuclear Electric Power and the Proliferation of Nuclear Weapon States," *International Security*, Vol. 1 (1977), pp. 98–99.

[42] Bertrand Goldschmidt, *supra* note 36, p. 70, p. 72.

Another factor prompting nonproliferation policy change stemmed from evolving U.S. national interests. Specifically, the realization that nuclear energy encompassed civilian economic potential, not just military concerns. This facilitated understanding that exporting U.S. power reactors could yield complementary economic gains. President Eisenhower's 1953 "Atoms for Peace" speech marking this policy shift[43] proposed creating the International Atomic Energy Agency (IAEA) to facilitate international civilian nuclear cooperation while managing proliferation risks.

2.3.2 From Technology Denial to Atoms for Peace: Uncertainty and Ambiguity

Through "Atoms for Peace," international nuclear cooperation was encouraged under a peaceful-use-only condition for accessing nuclear technology.[44] A liberal policy did not limit international cooperation to applications of the U.S. light water reactor technology, which was less proliferation-risky. This policy also permits international cooperation using the Canadian heavy water type reactor or in some "sensitive" fields involving plutonium reprocessing and uranium enrichment. Making a clear-cut distinction of what constituted "peaceful" technology was difficult due to potential proliferation risk. Indeed, even the light water reactor technology became a proliferation concern in the 1970s.[45]

In uranium manufacture, a strict control policy continued. In the preceding section, the nonproliferation merits of the strict control over uranium enrichment technology were discussed. The view that controlling uranium enrichment technology could prevent the production of highly enriched uranium useful for making atomic bombs has been widely accepted. Further, control over uranium enrichment technology can help reduce proliferation risk from plutonium produced through a light water reactor.[46] The promotion of light water reactors[47] and control over the dissemination

---

[43] U.N. Doc. A/PV.470, U.N. GAOR, 8th Sess., 450th Plenary Meeting, p. 450 (1953).

[44] Statute of the International Atomic Energy Agency art. 2, opened for signature Oct. 26, 1956, entered into force July 29, 1957, 276 U.N.T.S. 4.

[45] For this view that emerged and gained influence in the 1970s, see Victor Gillinsky, "Restraining the Spread of Nuclear Weapons: A Walk on the Supply Side," in Jed C. Snyder ed., *Limiting Nuclear Proliferation* (Ballinger Pub. Co., 1985), pp. 266–268.

[46] The fuel for the light water reactor consists of low-enriched uranium (approximately 3% enrichment). By controlling enrichment technology, the United States maintains significant influence over the global low-enriched uranium supply. Any operation of light water reactors aimed at manufacturing weapon-usable plutonium can be readily identified by an abrupt, unexplained increase in low-enriched uranium demand beyond what is justified for peaceful energy needs.

[47] By the mid-1970s, in the sixty nuclear reactors exported from the United States, the U.S. Export–Import Bank financed fifty of them and only three small reactors exported to Europe in the 1960s were carried out without any financial subsidy. See Congress, House, Committee on International Relations, Subcommittee on International Security and Scientific Affairs, Nuclear Proliferation: Future U.S. Foreign Policy Implications, Hearing before the Subcommittee on International Security

of enrichment technology were most critical to the success of the "Atoms for Peace" policy.[48]

However, because uranium enrichment technology is crucial for manufacturing the fuel used in light water reactors, the more the U.S. promoted its light water reactors, the stronger became the pressure from recipient states to relax controls over uranium enrichment technology. Fearing that the United States would control their nuclear power industry, recipient states sought more freedom in fuel manufacture, especially in the field of uranium enrichment manufacture. Under such circumstances, maintaining strict controls would prove difficult, yet defining enrichment policy without nuance could also be undesirable.

The U.S. nonproliferation policy on plutonium reprocessing was slightly different from that on uranium enrichment. It was less stringent for two reasons. First, Canada and France had succeeded in developing the solvent extraction method for plutonium extraction, and this technology had been widely disseminated to developed countries through the 1955 Conference on the Peaceful Use of Atomic Energy.[49] Second, plutonium reprocessing technology was not directly connected to the U.S. strategy of promoting light water reactors.

In practice, the United States government took a discriminatory approach to reprocessing technology, which also led to policy ambiguity that helped conceal the discrimination. For example, the United States was particularly tolerant of, if not supportive toward, its two closed allies in Asia and Europe—Japan and West Germany—regarding access to reprocessing technology. In October 1956, the U.S. Atomic Energy Commission (AEC) decided to allow Japan to research extracting plutonium from a small amount of nuclear waste.[50] A Japanese reprocessing plant designed and built with the assistance from Great Britain and France in the late 1960s faced no opposition. In the case of West Germany, the United States did not object to German indigenous development in the sensitive nuclear field and undertook cooperative research with the latter. The United States exported 355 kg of plutonium to Euratom, which may share it with West Germany within the Euratom framework.[51]

---

and Scientific Affairs, 95th Cong., 1st Sess., 100. Cited in Clarence D. Long, "Nuclear Proliferation: Can Congress Act in Time?" *International Security*, Vol. 1 (1977), p. 55.

[48] A subordinate policy in the field of uranium involved exerting influence over international natural uranium supplies. It is reported that by the end of 1970, the United States, Canada and South Africa collectively held approximately 80% of the proven uranium ore reserves in the "free world." By contracting purchase agreements with Canada and South Africa, United States strongly influenced the conditions under which such natural uranium should be sold to third states from these two countries. See Lawrence Scheinman, "Security and a Transnational System: The Case of Nuclear Energy," *International Organization*, Vol. 25 (1971), pp. 637–638.

[49] Bertrand Goldschmidt, *supra* note 36, p. 72.

[50] Genshiryoku Iinkai (JAEC), ed., *Genshiryoku Kaihatsu 30 Nen Shi (Thirty-year History of Nuclear Development)* (Genshiryoku Iinkai, 1986), p. 491. Cited in Motoya Kitamura, "Japan's Plutonium Program: A Proliferation Threat?" *The Nonproliferation Review*, Vol. 3 (1996), p. 4.

[51] Glenn T. Seaborg, Letter from the AEC Chairman Glenn T. Seaborg to Special Assistant to the President for National Security Affairs McGeorge Bundy (Sept. 30, 1964), in Nuclear Non-Proliferation: Declassified Documents, vol. 1, doc. 996 (National Security Archive 1991).

In contrast, although the United States entered a bilateral nuclear cooperation agreement immediately after "Atoms for Peace" announcement with Turkey, one of its NATO allies, no substantial nuclear cooperation was implemented between the two countries. Turkey even failed to obtain any nuclear assistance from other western countries due to objections from the U.S. government. Argentina and Brazil each imported one nuclear power plant from the United States but were denied sensitive technologies by the U.S. government.[52]

2.3.3 Normative Factors and the Concept of Peaceful Use of Nuclear Energy: Cases of Japan and Germany

In the period of recovery after the Second World War, Japan and West Germany were ambitious in developing nuclear power industry to meet their domestic energy needs. However, both Japan and Germany were defeated by the United Nations in the recent war and prohibited from remilitarizing immediately afterwards. As such, nuclear issues were viewed as extremely sensitive matters in the two countries.

While their recent wartime defeat limited remilitarization, as sovereign states within the international community, Japan and West Germany did not appear normatively prohibited from pursuing nuclear capabilities. As major beneficiaries of the Atoms for Peace policy, the two countries supported a more liberal policy for peaceful use of nuclear energy—both domestically and internationally. Because domestic laws in the countries restricted nuclear activities to peaceful application (as subsequently discussed), endorsing sensitive activities under the label of "peaceful use" became necessary to satisfy restrictions at home. In doing so, they strongly aimed to legitimize indigenous nuclear fuel cycle and nuclear exports as falling into the scope of the peaceful use of nuclear energy.

The fundamental principle of Japanese nuclear policy can be found in the Atomic Energy Basic Law of 1956: "The research, development and utilization of atomic energy shall be limited to peaceful purposes."[53] Under this law, "dual regimes" were established for the peaceful use of nuclear energy: one was a "utilization" regime and another a "development and research regime."[54] They referred to different projects under separate governmental administrations. "Utilization" related more to foreign assistance, mainly from the United States and Britain, with commercial nuclear power applications. This project fell under the regulation of the Ministry of International Trade and Industry (MITI). "Development and research" involved indigenous efforts in fields like reprocessing and uranium enrichment less likely

[52] This situation later contributed to unsuccessful cooperation efforts between these two states and Germany and France. The latter countries had promised to supply power reactors and sensitive nuclear technologies as components of their supply packages.

[53] Atomic Energy Basic Law of 1956, Law No. 186, art. 2 (Japan).

[54] Hitoshi Yoshioka, *Genshiryoku No Syakaishi: So No Nihon No Tenkai* (*The Social History of Nuclear Power: Its Development in Japan*) (Asahi Sinbunsha, 1999), pp. 18–28.

to obtain foreign aid. This project was under the jurisdiction of the Science and Technology Agency.

Whereas private electric power companies played decisive roles in the nuclear power station business under the "utilization" regime, "development and research" was carried out by state-run enterprises. These included the Japan Atomic Energy Research Institute (JAERI), NIHON NENRYOU KOUSHA—the predecessor of the Power Reactor and Nuclear Fuel Development Corporation (PNC), and the Institute of Physical and Chemical Research (IPCR). They were the so-called "TOKUSHU HOUJIN" (corporations with special legal status) under the jurisdiction of the Science and Technology Agency. By placing research and development under governmental oversight, Japan paved the way to acquiring capacity in plutonium reprocessing and uranium enrichment.

In the early period of Japanese nuclear development, policy priority was given to "utilization." Japan's engagement in the peaceful use of nuclear energy was symbolized by its rapid growth in constructing nuclear power reactors for electricity generation purposes, with assistance from Great Britain and the United States.[55] However, "development and research" received balanced policy considerations. In the first Long Term Program of 1956, the Japan Atomic Energy Commission (JAEC) decided that the development of a complete indigenous fuel cycle as well as breeder reactors represented the basic policy of the Japanese long-term nuclear program.[56] In the third "Long Term Program" (1967), JAEC specified this basic policy further by treating its domestic nuclear fuel cycle as an "essential" part of the nuclear program and initiating related projects.

In the field of fuel reprocessing, Japan Atomic Energy Research Institute (JAERI) started a research program in 1957 and carried out a hot test on its experimental reprocessing facility in March 1968. During one year of operation, it produced 208 g of purified plutonium.[57] In parallel, efforts sought foreign assistance. In 1962, the JAEC issued a report suggesting establishing a reprocessing plant by importing commercially available foreign technology. In February 1966, a contract for a complete design of a reprocessing plant was made with France.[58]

In the field of uranium enrichment, Japan carried out research and development through indigenous effort. The Institute of Physical and Chemical Research (IPCR) started research on a gas centrifuge process for uranium enrichment. This research project was later transferred to NIHON NENRYOU KOUSHA (the predecessor of the Power Reactor and Nuclear Fuel Development Corporation (PNC) under the

---

[55] Akatuki Takayanagi, "Nihon No Genshiryoku Sangyo No Tenkai" (The Development of Japanese Nuclear Energy Industry), in Saitou Yuu, Satou Eiichi eds., *Kaku Enerugi Seisaku (Nuclear Energy Policy)* (The Japan Institute of International Affairs, 1979), pp. 183–190.

[56] Eugene Skolnikoff, Tatsujiro Suzuki, Kenneth Oye, *International Responses to Japanese Plutonium Programs* (Working Paper from the Center for International Studies, Massachusetts Institute of Technology, August 1995), p. 2.

[57] Hitoshi Yoshioka, *supra* note 54, p. 109.

[58] *Ibid.*, p. 122.

1961 Long Term Program.[59] In August 1978, PNC successfully started a uranium enrichment operation in a pilot plant using a gas centrifuge process at Ningyo Toge.[60]

In West Germany, the federal Atomic Energy Act explicitly stated that the purpose of German nuclear activity is to "further nuclear research and development and the use of nuclear energy for peaceful purpose."[61] Similar to Japan, the nuclear fuel cycle was considered a crucial part of West Germany's peaceful use of nuclear energy. West Germany embarked on constructing an integrated nuclear fuel cycle center at Gorleben with facilities for the storage, reprocessing, refabrication of fuel, and for the conditioning and final disposal of waste.[62]

Japan and West Germany were two major clients of U.S. supplies of light water reactors. For these two countries to establish indigenous nuclear fuel cycles including uranium enrichment and plutonium reprocessing was natural as more nuclear reactors were built. Regardless of apparent peaceful use policies in the two countries, the U.S. government viewed sensitive nuclear activities in them as proliferation-prone. The U.S. State Department and the U.S. Arms Control and Disarmament Agency (ACDA) concluded in 1964 and 1965 that Japan was technologically and economically capable of becoming a major nuclear-weapon state within six years.[63] For West Germany, the United States assessed in 1964 that it already had the capacity to produce weapon-usable plutonium.[64]

In the pre-NPT era, "going nuclear" by manufacturing nuclear weapons was generally considered an appropriate national prerogative. States saw little need to justify indigenous nuclear activities as solely for "peaceful use" unless required to assure so by supplier states. However, with a treaty proposed that could normatively prohibit "going nuclear," sensitive peaceful nuclear activities that were previously viewed as appropriate became questionable. The shift in appropriateness frustrated efforts in Japan and West Germany to define a clear and extensive scope for peaceful nuclear activities.

Before discussing views on manufacturing nuclear weapons, it is important to first distinguish perspectives regarding the use of nuclear weapons from those relating to the manufacture of nuclear weapons.

---

59 The IPCR also succeeded in experimentally enriching uranium through the gaseous diffusion process after transferring the gas centrifuge project to the PNC. See Hitoshi Yoshioka, *supra* note 54, p. 124. In addition to the government-led research efforts, Asahi Kasei also independently achieved uranium enrichment at the laboratory scale through chemical exchange methods. See Akatuki Takayanagi, *supra* note 55, p. 200.

60 Hitoshi Yoshioka, *supra* note 54, p. 124.

61 Act on the Peaceful Use of Atomic Energy and Protection against its Hazards, December 23, 1959, Sect. 1(1), reprinted in *Nuclear Law Bulletin* No. 4 Supplement (1969), p. 3.

62 Thomas Roser, "Nuclear Energy and International Relations: The Case for the Federal Republic of Germany," *American Society of International Law Proceedings*, Vol. 73 (1979), p. 171.

63 "Background Paper on Factors Which Could Influence National Decision Concerning Acquisitions of Nuclear Weapons," Department of State, December 12, 1964 (Document No. 1079), in Nuclear Non-Proliferation Declassified Documents, (National Security Archive, 1991), pp. 12–16; "Memorandum for the Members of the Committee of Principals," ACDA, June 25, 1965 (Document No. 1807) in Declassified Documents 1994 (Research Publication, 1994), pp. 1–16.

64 Glenn T. Seaborg, *supra* note 51.

States have concluded treaties banning the use of certain types of weapons for humanitarian purposes, such as the Declaration of Saint Petersburg of 1868 which renounced employing any projectile under 400 g charged with explosive or inflammable substances in war.[65] Since the early 20th century, treaties have prohibited weapons made of specific materials to avoid inhumane effects.[66] Apart from treaty law, the use of some weapons, including nuclear weapons, may contravene rules of humanitarian law.[67] However, banning weapon use for humanitarian reasons does not automatically prohibit development, manufacturing, and deployment, as these acts do not directly raise humanitarian concerns.

What was Japan's position on "going nuclear?" One potential legal obstacle that prevents Japan from doing so was its "Peace Constitution." Article 9 (Renunciation of War) of the Japanese Constitution states:

> Aspiring sincerely to an international peace based on justice and order, the Japanese people forever renounce war as a sovereign right of the nation and the threat or use of force as the means of settling international disputes.
>
> To accomplish the aim of the preceding paragraph, land, sea, and air forces, as well as other war potential, will never be maintained. The right of belligerency of the state will not be recognized.

This article, especially the second paragraph, created uncertainty around whether Japan could legally acquire nuclear weapons. However, the apparent constitutional restriction did not prevent the Japanese Government from maintaining the position that Japan has the right to possess them.

The official stance was that acquiring nuclear weapons is not unconstitutional. However, for practical reasons, Japan did not intend to acquire them at the time but would not preclude doing so in the future. Prime Minister Ichiro Hatoyama first explicitly articulated this position in 1955, stating it was consistent with Article 9 of the Japanese Constitution to acquire nuclear arms for defensive purposes. He also noted that Japan had no plan to develop such weapons as long as American protection was assured.

---

65 Declaration of St. Petersburg (1868), available at <https://avalon.law.yale.edu/19th_century/decpeter.asp>.

66 Hague Declaration concerning Asphyxiating Gases (prohibited the use of asphyxiating or deleterious gases); Treaty relating to the Use of Submarines and Noxious Gases in Warfare, Washington, 6 February 1922 (prohibited the use of asphyxiating, poisonous or other gases, and all analogous liquids, materials or devices); Protocol for the Prohibition of the Use of Asphyxiating, Poisonous or Other Gases, and of Bacteriological Methods of Warfare. Geneva, 17 June 1925. (prohibited the use of asphyxiating, poisonous or other gases, all analogous liquids materials or devices, and bacteriological methods of warfare).

67 For example, in the *Legality of the Threat or Use of Nuclear Weapons (Advisory Opinion)*, the Court says in part 2 E: "the threat or use of nuclear weapons would generally be contrary to the rules of international law applicable in armed conflict, and in particular the principles and rules of humanitarian law. However, in view of the current state of international law, and of the elements of fact at its disposal, the Court cannot conclude definitively whether the threat or use of nuclear weapons would be lawful or unlawful in an extreme circumstance of self-defense, in which the very survival of a State would be at stake." See *Legality of the Threat or Use of Nuclear Weapons, Advisory Opinion*, I. C. J. Reports 1996, p. 226, para. 105.

In 1967, Prime Minister Eisaku Sato articulated the famouse "Three Nonnuclear Principles" (December 11, 1967), which described the policy of "not possessing, not producing and not permitting the introduction of nuclear weapons into Japan." However, the mere existence of this policy implies no statutory or constitutional prohibition on acquiring or manufacturing nuclear weapons. The "Three Nonnuclear Principles" merely repeated the 1955 Hatoyama Statement that Japan would not produce nuclear weapons for the time being. In 1970 when Japan signed the NPT, the government reaffirmed possessing small nuclear weapons was legally permissible if "within the minimum necessary limit of ability for self-defense, and not to constitute a threat of aggression toward other nations."[68]

Only after Japan ratified the NPT in 1976 was the right to acquire nuclear weapons viewed as having been deprived by the treaty. However, the official position implied the treaty restriction did not influence the constitutional status of acquiring nuclear weapons.[69] A Cabinet official to the Upper House of Parliament best summarized the official stance on the issue of constitutionality of possessing nuclear weapons in April 1982:

> The constitution does not prohibit the possession of war capability as long as it does not exceed the minimum required for self-defense. Therefore, the possession of weapons, whether nuclear or conventional, is not in itself prohibited insofar as it remains within the aforementioned limits. Nonetheless, we have chosen to abide by the policy of nonpossession of nuclear weapons in accordance with the Tree Nonnuclear Principle of our nation.[70]

The German position on "going nuclear" was more subtle than in Japan, where constitutionality dominated debate. For West Germany, the legal obstacle to possessing nuclear weapons stemmed from treaty obligations in the Paris Peace Agreements of 1954. As a defeated state in the Second World War, West Germany was temporarily deprived of sovereignty until protocols were concluded ending the occupation regime.[71] According to some provisions, West Germany was obliged

---

[68] *Nihon No Bōei (The Defense of Japan)* (Japan Defense Agency, 1970), p. 36.

[69] The Japanese government, upon signing the NPT on February 3, 1970, made the following statement: "5. The Government of Japan takes note of the fact that Article X of the Treaty provides that: 'each Party shall in exercising its national sovereignty have the right to withdraw from the Treaty if it decides that extraordinary events, related to the subject matter of this Treaty, have jeopardized the supreme interests of its country.'" See Japan: Signature of Treaty on the Non-Proliferation of Nuclear Weapons (NPT), available at <https://treaties.un.org/doc/Publication/UNTS/Volume%20729/v729.pdf>. By acknowledging this withdrawal provision, Japan indicated the "going nuclear" option could potentially be retrieved were treaty obligations to cease.

[70] "Statement by Reijiro Tsunoda, Director General of the Cabinent Legislation Bureau, to the Upper House Budget Committee, April 5, 1982," in *Proceedings of the Upper House Budget Committee* No. 20. Cited in Atsushi Tsuchida, "The Nuclear Arming of Japan," in William M Evan and Ved P. Nanda eds., *Nuclear Proliferation and the Legality of Nuclear Weapons* (University Press of America, 1995), p. 106.

[71] A series of protocols modifying and extending the Brussels Treaty of 1948 (Treaty of Economic, Social, and Cultural Collaboration and Collective Self-Defence, March 17, 1948) were signed at Paris on October 23, 1954. They are: Protocol Modifying and Completing the Brussels Treaty, [1955] 211 UNTS. 342; Protocol No. II on Forces of Western European Union, 211 UNTS 358; Protocol No. III on the Control of Armaments, 211 UNTS 364; Protocol No. IV on the Agency of Western

not to manufacture certain weapon types, including nuclear weapons. For example, Annex 1 of Protocol No. III on the Control of Armaments declared "… the Federal Republic undertakes not to manufacture in its territory any atomic weapons, chemical weapons or biological weapons, as detailed in paragraphs I, II and III of the attached list."[72]

To what extent would this treaty obligation influence West Germany's view on "going nuclear"? Two reasons suggest it may not have directly banned such an option. First, as a "peace treaty," historical precedents indicate such treaties weaken over time as relations normalize. Second, the manufacturing prohibition in the protocol contained loopholes open to interpretation. It could be argued research and development lay outside the ban.[73] Moreover, acquiring nuclear weapons from foreign suppliers was arguably not precluded. Therefore, West Germany may have maintained it retained the right to obtain these arms externally. Further, some interpret the territorial limitation as allowing cooperation with other states on weapons manufacture. Even with these postwar protocols, West Germany likely viewed "going nuclear" as an option not ruled out.

Japan and West Germany sought to clarify and expand the scope of permitted peaceful use of nuclear activities to include sensitive fields. In doing so, both states appeared to view "going nuclear" as an option still seen as appropriate. However, emerging NPT normatively prohibited nuclearization. Given this shift in appropriateness norms, the two countries aimed to lessen the treaty's impact on domestic nuclear programs. Toward this end, they examined ambiguities in the provisions defining the scope of prohibited activities.

2.4 Conclusion

Under the traditional principle of consent, states are motivated by self-interest and common interests to agree.[74] National interest and state consent are traditionally seen as pivotal in determining the provisions' content.[75] Consent assumes interests guide utility-maximizing decisions, without normative considerations of consent's propriety. It also assumes relatively stable interests exist. This view is

---

European Union for the Control of Armaments, 211 UNTS 376. Along with the execution of the four protocols to the Brussels Treaty, two further protocols were made to invite the West Germany into NATO: Protocol to the North Atlantic Treaty on the Accession of the Federal Republic of Germany, October 23, 1954, 243 UNTS 308; Protocol on the Termination of the Occupation Regime in the Federal Republic of Germany, October 23, 1954, 331 UNTS 253.

[72] Protocol No. III on the Control of Armaments, 211 UNTS 364.

[73] Mason Willrich, "West Germany's Pledge Not to Manufacture Nuclear Weapons," *Virginia Journal of International Law*, Vol. 7 (1966–1967), p. 94.

[74] Louis Henkin, *How Nations Behave: Law and Foreign Policy* (2nd ed., Columbia University Press, 1979), pp. 32–37; Anthony A. D'Amato, *The Concept of Custom in International Law* (Cornell University Press, 1971), p. 40.

[75] Fermando. R. Teson, *A Philosophy of International Law* (Westview Press, 1998), p. 73.

rationalist.[76] Constructivism challenges such assumptions. For example, Wendt noted interests are defined through social context, not exogenously held.[77] Recent work on the Rational Design of International Institution project[78] incorporated uncertainty and the logic of appropriateness into the understanding of the flexibility, helping explain emerging dynamic obligations through consent negotiations. This provides a more constructivist lens acknowledging interests' endogenous nature and consent's complex motivations.

Examining the pre-NPT nuclear nonproliferation regime's evolution suggests the primary factor behind designing ambiguities into the NPT stemmed from uncertainties around nuclear technology. Considering economic interests also comprised part of national interests calculations in this issue area. This gave the United States pause regarding the rigidity of its earlier nonproliferation policies by incorporating additional factors into analyses of its own interests.

The second source of dynamic obligations stems from normative appropriateness, as seen in the Japanese and German cases. As the largest beneficiaries of the "Atoms for Peace", both eagerly expanded the scope of permitted peaceful nuclear energy uses to include enrichment and reprocessing. Regardless of domestic restrictions, they viewed "going nuclear" as an option. The analysis showed this normative shift frustrated their efforts to clarify and broaden the scope of sensitive nuclear activities as "peaceful." This implied an important factor behind the NPT ambiguities: a sudden change from viewing "going nuclear" as appropriate to prohibited would lead states to reconsider clearly banning activities previously deemed acceptable. However, this shift risked opposition to prohibiting certain activities expended as "peaceful."

This pre-NPT survey illustrates sources of dynamic obligations in a nonproliferation treaty. Given these detected sources, it would be worthwhile to examine the actual NPT drafting process to discern how consensual treaty-making may achieve intentional ambiguity.

---

[76] Duncan Snidal, "The Game Theory of International Politics," in Kenneth A. Oye ed., *Cooperation Under Anarchy* (Princeton University Press, 1986), p. 43. (noting that rationalist theory makes sense in explaining state behavior only under an assumption that national interests and states' preferences remain stable over time).

[77] Alexander Wendt, "Anarchy Is What States Make of It," *International Organization*, Vol. 46, No. 2 (1992), p. 394.

[78] Barbara Koremenos, Charles Lipson and Duncan Snidal, *supra* note 4, p. 762. (noting that international institutions are defined as "explicit arrangements, negotiated among international actors, that prescribe, proscribe, and/or authorize behavior").

Chapter 3
The Making of Dynamic Obligations: The "Inalienable Right" and *Travaux Préparatoires* of the NPT

3.1 Introduction

This chapter will investigate the process of consent—the negotiating process and *travaux préparatoires* of the NPT. The main target of the analysis is the "inalienable right" as well as the "right to participate" in Article IV of the NPT. However, since the structure of the text of Article IV requires a contextual reading of Article II of the NPT, investigation will also focus on the drafting of the scope of the prohibited "manufacture" in Article II of the NPT.

This Chapter is an attempt to help to answer an immediate question in understanding the dynamic nature of treaty rules: how do states actually make dynamic obligations into a treaty? In answering this question, the author will revisit the NPT travaux préparatoires, aiming at building up a solid foundation for genuine interdisciplinary research on the role of international legal rules in international relations.[1] The Chapter will then investigate the NPT *travaux préparatoires* recorded in the United Nations Documents and Official Records[2] to see how ambiguity has been made on the wording of "inalienable right," "the right to participate," as well as the relevant wording of "manufacture" in Articles I and II.

[1] It should be pointed out that the present author is not using *travaux préparatoires* as a supplementary means of interpretation stipulated in Article 32 of the Vienna Convention on the Law of Treaties (VCLT), but rather to show an intentional design of ambiguous treaty provisions to allow for a "dynamic treaty obligation" wherein the "art" of treaty interpretation codified in the VCLT Article 31 fails to account for this.

[2] Collection held at the Kyoto United Nations Depository Library.

X. Zhang, *Law and Politics in Peaceful Use of Nuclear Energy*,
https://doi.org/10.1007/978-981-97-3813-7_3

3.2 The Right to Nuclear Weapons and the Right to Peaceful Use of Nuclear Energy: The Irish Proposals for a Shared Expectation

The making of the NPT started from the common concerns and expectations of international community on how to handle nuclear weapons. The Irish Delegation in a series of proposals and a series of resolutions passed by the UN General Assembly brought out the idea of nuclear nonproliferation that manufacturing of nuclear weapons should be prohibited. These proposals and resolutions forged a shared expectation of the majority of the international community in supporting an international agreement for nuclear nonproliferation.

The Irish Foreign Minister Frank Aiken articulated an original idea for a nuclear nonproliferation agreement in the General Conference (plenary session) of the 13th U.N. General Assembly on September 19, 1958. In his speech, Aiken set forth the idea that it was necessary to conclude an international agreement to put a ceiling on the number of nuclear-weapon states to the existing three countries (The U.S., U.S.S.R., and U.K., as of 1958). He suggested that the agreement would require non-nuclear-weapon states not to manufacture, purchase, receive, or possess nuclear weapons while nuclear-weapon states not to supply nuclear weapons to non-nuclear weapons states.[3]

Aiken's original nonproliferation idea prompted concrete steps. On Oct. 17, 1958, in the First Committee of the UN General Assembly, the Irish delegation proposed a draft calling upon "all states that are not now producing nuclear weapons to refrain from undertaking manufacture."[4] In November, 1959, the Irish delegation proposed and introduced a resolution in the General Assembly supporting an international agreement banning transfers of nuclear weapons.[5]

In 1960, the Irish nonproliferation proposal seemed not to insist on making an international nonproliferation agreement. Ireland proposed what subsequently became General Assembly Resolution 1576 (XV), jointly with Japan, Canada, Mexico and Morocco, calling upon "Powers not possessing such weapons, on a similar *temporary and voluntary basis*, to refrain from manufacturing these weapons and from otherwise attempting to acquire them."[6] (emphasis added). By using the wording "on …temporary and voluntary basis," the resolution implied that non-nuclear-weapon states did have the right of manufacturing nuclear weapons.

The last one of the series of the Irish proposals was made in 1961, in which the idea of 1958 Aiken speech to conclude an international agreement in preventing nuclear weapon proliferation revived. This proposal was adopted unanimously as Resolution 1665 (XVI), with the title "Prevention of the Wider Dissemination of Nuclear

---

[3] U.N. Doc. A/PV.751 (September 19, 1958), paras. 81–84.

[4] U.N. Doc. A/C.1/L.206 (October 17, 1958). This draft was proposed to revise a previously submitted draft of resolution on suspending nuclear test. However, the draft was later withdrawn before coming to a vote.

[5] U.N. Doc. GA Res 1380 (November 20, 1959).

[6] U.N. Doc. A/4680 (December 20, 1960), para. 10.

Weapons." This resolution called upon "all States, and in particular upon the States at present possessing nuclear weapons, to use their best endeavors to secure the conclusion of *an international agreement* containing provisions under which the nuclear States would undertake to refrain from relinquishing control of nuclear weapons and from transmitting the information necessary for their manufacture to States not possessing such weapons, and provisions under which States not possessing nuclear weapons would undertake not to manufacture or otherwise acquire control of such weapons."[7] (emphasis added).

The NPT was thus drafted in response to such a nonproliferation expectation. As the series of Irish proposals and relevant U.N. resolutions indicated, the legal status of non-nuclear-weapon states at that time was that all of these states had the right to develop nuclear weapons.[8] To agree to conclude an international agreement on nuclear nonproliferation means that non-nuclear-weapon states were ready to give up their right to manufacture as well as to receive nuclear weapons. However, unilateral denunciation of the right of acquiring nuclear weapons would give rise to concerns over asymmetrical security disadvantages as well as fear of losing benefits from peaceful use of nuclear energy. Security concerns are needed to be addressed and benefits from peaceful use of nuclear energy to be assured. In subsequent treaty negotiations, a "bargaining" structure was designed to meet such concerns from non-nuclear-weapon states. The concept of the inalienable right to the peaceful use of nuclear energy was articulated in such a context.[9] In the following sections, emphasis will be given on how the article on the inalienable right was forged in the NPT negotiation.

3.3 From Expectation to Substantive Provisions: Drafting the Ambiguity

In the following sections, the author will trace the riddle of the "inalienable right" through the study of *travaux préparatoires* and see how ambiguity was intentionally designed.

[7] U.N. Doc. GA Res 1665 (December 4, 1961).

[8] Even the originator of the concept of nonproliferation, Irish Foreign Minister Frank Aiken, acknowledged this point. See Frank Aiken, "Can We Limit the Nuclear Club?" *Bulletin of the Atomic Scientists*, Vol. 17 (1961), p. 265.

[9] Treaty on the Nonproliferation of Nuclear Weapons, opened for signature July 1, 1968, entered into force March 5, 1970, extended indefinitely by the 1995 NPT Review and Extension Conference), 729 UNTS 161. (Other compensations include: an undertaking to ensure "potential benefits from any peaceful applications of nuclear explosions will be made available to non-nuclear-weapon States Party to the Treaty" (Article V); an undertaking "to pursue negotiations in good faith on effective measures relating to cessation of the nuclear arms race at an early date and to nuclear disarmament, and on a treaty on general and complete disarmament under strict and effective international control" (Article VI)). Further, effective security guarantees were provided to protect States renouncing nuclear weapons from any threat of nuclear blackmail. See U.N. Doc. SC Res 255 (June 19, 1968).

3.3.1 *Incorporating the Inalienable Right in the NPT Drafts*

The first drafts respectively submitted by the United States[10] and by the Soviet Union[11] dealt exclusively with the prohibition of nuclear weapons. No bargaining provisions, such as those concerning the peaceful use of nuclear technology, were provided in either draft. The imbalance of the rights and obligations of non-nuclear-weapon states became a concern in the international community. Under the Non-Aligned Countries' initiative, Resolution 2028 (XX) was adopted by the General Assembly, which introduced certain principles to guide the ongoing treaty negotiation.[12] Among the principles, the treaty "should embody an acceptable balance of mutual responsibilities and obligations of the nuclear and non-nuclear Powers" and "should be a step towards the achievement of general and complete disarmament and, more particularly, nuclear disarmament."[13] Nevertheless, the right to the peaceful use of nuclear energy was not specified in the principles articulated in this resolution.

Shortly after that, the peaceful use of nuclear energy issue in the context of the NPT negotiation appeared in General Assembly Resolution 2156 (XXI). It said, "[The General Assembly] decides to convene a conference of non-nuclear-weapon Powers ... to consider ... (c) how can nuclear devices be used for exclusively peaceful purpose"?[14]

In addressing the concerns of non-nuclear-weapon states, the Soviet Union and the United States added, in the 1967 U.S.-Soviet Identical Draft presented to the Eighteen Nation Committee on Disarmament (ENDC), August 24, 1967, content on the right to the peaceful use of nuclear energy. The preamble of that draft contained two clauses on the matter:

> Affirming the principle that the benefits of peaceful applications of nuclear technology... should be available for peaceful purposes to all Parties to the Treaty ...
>
> Convinced that ... all parties to this Treaty are entitled to participate in the fullest possible exchange of scientific information for, and to contribute alone or in cooperation with other States to, the further development of the applications of atomic energy for peaceful purposes.[15]

This draft also provided a short version of the "inalienable right" clause matching the two paragraphs in the preamble. Article IV appeared in the draft as follows:

---

[10] "The U. S. Draft Treaty to Prevent the Spread of Nuclear Weapons, Aug. 17, 1965;" "Amendment to the U. S. Draft Treaty to Prevent the Spread of Nuclear Weapons, March 21, 1966." See U.N. Doc. A/5986 (August 17, 1965), annex I.

[11] "The U.S.S.R. Draft Treaty on the Nonproliferation of Nuclear Weapons, Sept. 24, 1965," See U.N. Doc. A/5976 (September 24, 1965), pp. 4–6. One notable difference between the two drafts is that the U.S. draft contained safeguard provision while the Soviet's Amendment omitted any mention of safeguards.

[12] U.N. Doc. GA Res 2028 (November 23, 1965).

[13] *Ibid.*, para. 2(b)(c).

[14] U.N. Doc. GA Res 2156 (November 22, 1966) Rev. 1, part B, para. 2(c).

[15] U.N. Doc. ENDC/192, 193 (August 24, 1967), p. 1.

> Nothing in this Treaty shall be interpreted as affecting the inalienable right of all the parties to the Treaty to develop, research, production and use of nuclear energy for peaceful purposes without discrimination and in conformity with Articles I and II of this Treaty, as well as the *right of the Parties to participate* in the fullest possible exchange of information for, and to contribute alone or in co-operation with other States to, the further development of the application of nuclear energy for peaceful purposes.[16] (emphasis added).

This drafted article, according to U.S. representative William Foster, was suggested by non-nuclear weapon countries. The wording of the article was borrowed from Article 17 of the Treaty of Tlateloco.[17]

3.3.2 *Article IV in the Final Draft Article*

Several proposals had been made to modify the identical draft of August 1967. Mexico proposed an idea to split Article IV into two paragraphs.[18] The purpose of making the "right to participate in the fullest possible exchange" an independent paragraph was to reinforce such a right in addition to the "inalienable right." Others saw the possible inconsistency between the "inalienable right" and "in conformity with Articles I and II," as well as insufficiency in the "right to participate." They proposed for clarification and urged concreteness.[19]

On January 18, 1968, the U.S. and the Soviet Union jointly submitted the third version of the NPT draft.[20] In the draft, the idea of splitting the Article IV of 1967 Draft was adopted. However, proposals for doing relevant clarification were turned down. The third version draft Article IV became the prototype of the treaty text. On March 11, 1968, with slight technical changes in paragraph 2, Article IV appears in the final version and prescribes:

1. Nothing in this Treaty shall be interpreted as affecting the inalienable right of all the Parties to the Treaty to develop research, production and use of nuclear energy for peaceful purposes without discrimination and in conformity with Articles I and II of this Treaty.
2. All the Parties to the Treaty (inserted at the final text "undertake to facilitate, and") have the right to participate in, the fullest possible exchange of (inserted at the final text "equipment, materials and") scientific and technological information for the peaceful uses of nuclear energy. Parties to the Treaty in a position to

---

[16] *Ibid.*, p. 3.

[17] U.N. Doc. ENDC/PV.325, para. 17. Article 17 of the Treaty of Tlateloco provides: "Nothing in the provisions of this Treaty shall prejudice the rights of the Contracting Parties, in conformity with this Treaty, to use nuclear energy for peaceful purposes, in particular for their economic development and social progress." See Treaty for the Prohibition of Nuclear Weapons in Latin America, opened for signature February 14, 1967, entered into force April 25, 1969, 634 UNTS 362, art. 17.

[18] U.N. Doc. ENDC/196 (September 19, 1967).

[19] See below Sect. 3.4.

[20] The text of 1968 Joint Draft was reprinted in *International Legal Materials*, Vol. 7(1968), pp. 155–161.

do so shall also co-operate in contributing alone or together with other States or international organizations to the further development of the applications of nuclear energy for peaceful purposes, especially in the territories of non-nuclear-weapon States Party to the Treaty. (added the last sentence in the final text "with due consideration for the needs of the developing areas of the world").[21]

The co-authors submitted the final draft of the NPT on behalf of the Eighteen Nation Committee on Disarmament (ENDC) to the U.N. General Assembly and the U.N. Disarmament Commission on March 14, 1968.[22] In the deliberation on the NPT draft carried by the First Committee of the General Assembly between April and June of 1968, Article IV was kept unchanged. On June 12, 1968, the General Assembly adopted the resolution recommending the Treaty.[23]

3.4 Deliberation by States: Efforts for Clarification versus Insistence on Ambiguity

With regard to the terms "inalienable right" and "right to participate," many States participated in the negotiation had fears for a contradiction between "inalienable right" and "in conformity with Articles I and II of this Treaty." They also showed concerns about the woolly conception of "right to participate."

3.4.1 Clarifying the "Inalienable Right"

Mexico, a sponsor of the Treaty of Tlateloco, indicated its understanding of this copied "right" that the provisions of the Treaty as a whole should not affect such right. Mexican delegation stated: "The first is the right to develop research, production and use of nuclear energy. To preclude an interpretation by which the Nuclear Nonproliferation Treaty might conflict with such acts, this right is expressed in a negative form, which amounts simply to legal interpretation of the provisions of the treaty as a whole: nothing in the treaty may be interpreted as affecting this right, which is called inalienable."[24]

Foster, the U.S. representative for negotiating the NPT in the Eighteen Nation Committee on Disarmament, stated, "... it makes clear that nothing in the draft treaty interferes with the right of the parties to develop their research, production and use of nuclear energy for peaceful purpose in compliance with Articles I and

---

21 Text of Draft on the Nonproliferation of Nuclear Weapons presented on 11 March 1968 (with the original notes on the changes to the January draft), Article IV. See *ibid.*, p. 567.

22 *Ibid.*, p. 563.

23 U.N. Doc. GA Res 2373 (June 18, 1968).

24 U.N. Doc. ENDC/PV.331, para. 7.

II."[25] Foster's statement merely repeated the text of the 1967 drafted article and did not touch upon the problem of possible contradiction between the "inalienable right" and "compliance with Articles I and II". On the latter point, Foster continued, "These provisions make it clear that the treaty would promote, not discourage, national development and international cooperation with respect to peaceful application of atomic energy. This applies to research, production and use as well as to information, equipment and material."[26] The continued part of the statement could be understood as siding with the Mexican position that the Treaty as a whole, including Articles I and II, would not lower the level of permissible nuclear activities for peaceful purposes. However, other countries seemed not to be as confident as Mexico on the possible contradiction with the "inalienable right" on the one hand and "in conformity with Articles I and II of this Treaty" on the other hand. The fear from non-nuclear-weapon states was that their "inalienable right" might be restricted by Article II: because Article II prohibited them from manufacturing nuclear weapons, some manufacturing activities could no longer be exercised.

Concerns about improper restriction on the "inalienable right" by a wide scope of prohibition on manufacture were not groundless. Indeed, in the 1965 Soviet Union draft, Article II did not only prohibit manufacturing but also "prepare [preparing] for the manufacture [of nuclear weapons]."[27] Although the word "prepare" was deleted in the 1967 identical draft, the scope of "manufacture" is still vague since the article did not specify which phase of nuclear activity should be interpreted as covered by the prohibition of "manufacture." Did it mean manufacture of plutonium or enriched uranium? What grade of enrichment, for example, the low-enrichment or high-enrichment, if outlawed, should it be? Did it mean manufacture of non-nuclear parts of a nuclear bomb? Or did it mean the final assembly of nuclear explosive device? In revising "prepare for the manufacture" and re-drafting "manufacture" in the 1967 U.S.-Soviet Union identical draft, the co-authors ostensibly aimed to preclude an outright ban on manufacturing preparation. However, what was the final phase of "manufacture" remained unclear.

The Swiss government worked on clarifying "manufacture" by enumerating certain "sensitive" nuclear activities as not to fall into the scope of the prohibited manufacturing. In an *aide-memoire* to the 1967 identical draft, Switzerland requested such an interpretation to be confirmed formally: "the phrase 'to manufacture or otherwise acquire nuclear weapons or other nuclear explosive devices' does not cover, according to the interpretation of the Swiss authorities, exploitation of uranium deposits, enrichment of uranium, extraction of plutonium from nuclear fuels, or manufacture of fuel elements of heavy water, when these processes are carried out for civil purposes."[28]

---

[25] U.N. Doc. ENDC/PV.325, para. 17.

[26] *Ibid.*, para. 18.

[27] U.S.S.R. Draft Treaty on the Nonproliferation of Nuclear Weapons, Sept. 24, 1965, *supra* note 11, p. 5.

[28] U.N. Doc. ENDC/204 (November 24, 1967), para. (1)(b).

Knowing well the concerns from non-nuclear-weapon states, the two co-authoring nuclear-weapon states, tried on many occasions to ease such fears. The Soviet Union, facing the proposals made by non-nuclear-weapon states for revising Article IV of the 1967 draft,[29] announced, "we base ourselves on the assumption that a treaty ... should enable [non-nuclear-weapon states] to develop their peaceful atomic industries and *all forms* of the peaceful use of nuclear energy."[30] (emphasis added). The United States delegate to the Eighteen Nation Committee also emphasized that the fear for an expanded interpretation was not well founded. Foster pointed out, "For example, the United States, as well as some other advanced civilian nuclear Powers, have made available materials and technology for the building of nuclear reactors, the fact that these reactors produce plutonium that can be used in weapons has not prevented us from supplying these materials and technology under adequate safeguards."[31] He further stressed, "A non-proliferation treaty which prohibits the manufacture or acquisition of nuclear explosive would not restrict the dissemination of application technology *in any fashion*."[32] (emphasis added). Moreover, in the general debate in the First Committee from April to May of 1968, Foster's explanation was repeated and confirmed by the U.S. delegation that the Treaty would not affect the right to the peaceful use of nuclear energy as far as nuclear material subject to safeguards designed to prevent diversion of such nuclear material into nuclear weapons.[33] The U.S. assured the States that the Treaty would "open wider the door to the benign use of atom."[34]

Nevertheless, statements of both the Soviets and the U.S. had a strong propaganda smell. They might help to alleviate the fear of non-nuclear-weapon states and lower the huddle for those states in adopting the treaty draft as well as joining the Treaty, but helped little in substantially clarifying the issue. On the contrary, the wording such as "all forms" or "in any fashion" caused confusion in understanding the scope of prohibition. The fundamental reason was that, every country realized that the non-proliferation obligation and the right of peaceful use needed to be balanced at certain point but no country, including the two co-authoring countries, knew where the balance point should be made. To ensure the success of treaty drafting as well as a wider acceptance of the Treaty from non-nuclear-weapon states, the only thing that the co-authors of the drafts could do was to pack the deal with rhetoric words.

Another salient example of such a "packing" was on choosing the word "inalienable right" in the draft. When copying Article 17 of the Treaty of Tlateloco into Article IV of the NPT, the word "inalienable" was added. Thus a plain "right" in Tlateloco was polished into "inalienable right" in the NPT. But was there any special meaning for using "inalienable right" instead of "right"? The answer is no. Investigation on the "manufacture" problem in Article II shows that the lip-service by adding

---

[29] Modifications were proposed by Brazil and Italy, see *infra* notes 35–36 and accompanying text.

[30] U.N. Doc. ENDC/PV.339, p. 6.

[31] U.N. Doc. ENDC/PV.303, para. 13.

[32] *Ibid.*, para. 18.

[33] U.N. Doc. A/C.1/PV.1556 (April 26, 1968), paras. 55–58.

[34] *Ibid.*, para. 54.

"inalienable" in front of the "right" did not help in safeguarding "inalienable right" from possible restriction coming from the wording "in conformity with Articles I and II of this Treaty."

Notwithstanding the ambiguity surrounding Article II, efforts toward clarifying Article IV had been made. The Brazilian Delegation proposed amendments to the 1967 August Draft and 1968 January Draft to delete the word "in conformity with Articles I and II of this Treaty."[35] The Italian Delegation suggested adding a new sentence to specify certain activities to be incorporated within the scope of the "inalienable right." Under its proposal, such activities should include those "to acquire source and special fissionable materials or equipment for the use of source and special fissionable materials for peaceful purposes."[36]

These two suggested clarifications were rejected by the co-authors. However, the concern from Italian delegation was reflected in the General Assembly Resolution recommending the final text of the Treaty. The resolution states that "Convincing that, pursuant to the provisions of the treaty, all signatories have the right to engage in research, production and use of nuclear energy for peaceful purpose and will be able to acquire source and special fissionable materials as well as equipment for the processing, use and production of nuclear for peaceful purposes."[37] This is, as we all well know, not binding on the parties to the NPT.

3.4.2 *On the "Right to Participate"*

As indicated above, the "right to participate" in paragraph 2 of Article IV came from a dichotomy of Article IV in the 1967 identical draft. Did the division of Article IV bring about special legal significance to the "right to participate"? President Johnson once indicated his understanding on Article IV (2) of the NPT: the United States would share its technical knowledge in peaceful nuclear research fully, and "without reservation."[38]

Indeed, some negotiating States understood that there might be a need for a parallel judiciary commitment to ensure the "right to participate." Mexico thus suggested, "[T]hose parties that are in a position to do so, have the *duty* to contribute, alone or in cooperation with other States or international organizations to the further development of the production, industries, and other applications of nuclear energy for peaceful purposes, especially in the territories of non-nuclear-weapon States."[39] (emphasis added). The Swiss government in its *aide-memoire* on Nov. 24, 1967 proposed a similar suggestion to incorporate such a juridical commitment in the

[35] U.N. Doc. ENDC/201 (October 31, 1967); U.N. Doc. ENDC/201/Rev.2 (February 13, 1968).

[36] U.N. Doc. ENDC/218 (February 20, 1968).

[37] See *supra* note 23.

[38] United States Arms Control and Disarmament Agency, International Negotiation on the Treaty on the Nonproliferation of Nuclear Weapons, January 1969, p. 125.

[39] U.N. Doc. ENDC/196 (September 19, 1967).

body of the treaty. It stated, "... the sixth paragraph of the preamble expressed the intention of the nuclear-weapon States to make available to all Parties ... the knowledge and benefits of nuclear technology ... capable of civil use. This intention should be transformed into a juridical commitment in the body of the Treaty."[40]

Objections to the proposed parallel judiciary commitment came from delegations of some developed countries with advanced nuclear technology. Canada and the United Kingdom argued that the term "duty" was too broad and could be interpreted to mean that any request from any non-nuclear-weapon state must be met.[41] The United States thought the nature of "duty" would be "too sweeping and too general," and stated, "We believe that this duty can and should be enunciated as a true legal obligation, although the obligation is imperfect and general and its practical significance will continue to depend ultimately on the will of the nuclear Powers."[42] These objections made Mexico, who proposed to insert "duty," realized that in practice, the duty would depend on the will of nuclear Powers.[43]

As a result, the proposed insertion of "duty" in matching the "right to participate" was rejected. However, paragraph 2, though lacking an autonomous and concrete legal significance, its hortatory language was considered to be useful in hiding the discriminative nature of the Treaty as well as reducing discontent from non-nuclear-weapon states. The co-authors used paragraph 2 as an "eye-catcher" when promoting the "sales" of the NPT. The United States representative made an impassioned speech on paragraph 2 of Article IV:

> On behalf of the United States and with the full authority of my Government, I *pledge* in this open forum and before this important committee of the Assembly unreservedly that, in keeping with the letter and spirit of this treaty provision, we will *appropriately and equitably* share our knowledge and experience, acquired at great cost, concerning all aspects of peaceful uses of nuclear energy, with the parties to the treaty, particularly the non-nuclear parties. This is not only a promise; when this treaty takes effect it will become an *obligation* under a treaty which, when approved by our Congress and President, will be, under our Constitution, a part of the supreme law of the land.[44] (emphasis added).

However, this rhetorical statement did not mean any change of the U.S. position in opposing an autonomous international obligation accompanying the "right to participate" in paragraph 2. By adding rhetoric tone into a plain text, the United States would implement the provision in a manner not obligatory but appropriate and equitable. It was to a great extent a matter of pledge or discretion.

The rhetorical paragraph 2 seemed to have only a limited effect. When deliberating paragraph 2 of Article IV, the Spanish representative felt that providing for the sharing of knowledge and experience in peaceful use of nuclear energy should be made more specific.[45] Likewise, the Argentine representative wished to turn them [provisions

---

[40] Supra note 28, para. (3)(a).

[41] Edwin Brown Firmage, "The Treaty on the Non-Proliferation of Nuclear Weapons," *American Journal of International Law*, Vol. 63 (1969), p. 728.

[42] U.N. Doc. ENDC/PV.338, para. 16.

[43] U.N. Doc. ENDC/PV.331, para. 11.

[44] U.N. Doc. A/C.1/PV.1556 (April 26, 1968), para. 53.

[45] U.N. Doc. A/C.1/PV.1569 (May 16, 1968), para. 156.

under Article IV and Article V] into effective and specific obligations. However, he left his wish to "the future by instruments clearly establishing how and in what measure the nuclear States is to cooperate in the advancement of nuclear science in the less developed countries."[46]

3.5 Conclusion

The investigation starts from the Irish proposals for the making of the NPT. As a normal step of cultivating an expectation deemed worthy of formal treaty coverage, the Irish proposals only forged a shared expectation without specifying any suggestion for the details of the treaty. This task was left to the treaty drafting. However, the investigation on the four versions of drafts of the NPT submitted by the co-authors of the U.S. and the Soviet Union indicates that the co-authors failed to make the relevant draft articles out of ambiguity.

Further discussion on states' positions in the drafting period as well as the deliberating meetings shows that states had chances and made efforts to clarify the relevant ambiguous provisions. However, a debate about the efforts for clarification vs. insistence on ambiguity shows that motivation of drafting of ambiguity remains. The ambiguity survives amidst a need of propaganda for a wide acceptance of the treaty and a must of maintaining more individual controls of dominant states over the treaty. The adoption of the ambiguous draft implies that even states struggled for clarity seemed to be contented with the ambiguity.

The investigation shows that language, due to its nature of indeterminacy, can be intentionally used in drafting an ambiguous treaty text, and this is the case of making the NPT Article IV. Concerning the first paragraph of Article IV, efforts to clarify the scope of the "inalienable right" were offset by the insistence on ambiguity. Similarly, proposals of autonomous obligation to match the right in the second paragraph were rejected. Article IV as a whole to a great extent only has hortatory significance. It did not establish specific and concrete legal rights and obligations. Professor Greig once observed the NPT drafting process and commented:

> Given the fact that the NPT deals with an area in which the vital interests of contracting States are of paramount importance, it would hardly be surprising to discover that the Treaty as a whole, as well as many of its provisions, gloss over potential areas of conflict in forms of wording which create the impression that agreement has been achieved and translated into legal prescriptions. Thus, in approaching the problem of interpreting the Treaty's provisions, it is necessary to bear in mind that 'the intention of the parties' might well include a deliberate choice in favor of accepting a text that gives an illusion, rather than a reality, of agreement. The reasons for adopting such a policy would include the belief that any treaty which establishes certain minimum undertakings is better than no treaty.[47]

---

[46] U.N. Doc. A/C.1/PV.1572 (May 22, 1968), para. 86.

[47] D. W. Greig, "The Interpretation of Treaties and Article IV.2 of the Nuclear Non-Proliferation Treaty," *Australian Yearbook of International Law*, Vol. 6 (1974–1975), p. 82.

In other words, treaty can be made, as the parties intended, to be ambiguous and thus difficult to operationalize in practice. In the case of the NPT negotiation, even countries that made efforts to clarify the draft, eventually found them satisfied, or compromised with the ambiguity. The NPT negotiation also shows a strong intention of the dominant players (such as the United States) in advocating such an ambiguity. The intentionally drafted ambiguity seemed to be tolerated by dissenting countries. For them, "an imperfect treaty is preferable to no treaty at all."[48]

Article 31 of Vienna Convention on the Law of Treaties is based on a proposition that there existed a clear legislative intention and thus an "interpretable" treaty provision. However, as this study disclosed, in international legislation this proposition is not always valid. It is maybe the time to rethink the "art" of treaty interpretation in resolving the riddle of the "inalienable right" as part of a "living, dynamic regime" which should be "capable of evolving to match changing realities."[49] To this point, further interdisciplinary study[50] on international legal rules in general as well as in finding a new "art" for treaty interpretation seems to be urgent and challenging.

[48] U.N. Doc. ENDC/PV/304, p. 10.

[49] Statements of IAEA Director General Dr. Mohamed ElBaradei in 2005 Review Conference of the Treaty on the Non-Proliferation of Nuclear Weapons, (May 2, 2005), available at <https://www.iaea.org/newscenter/statements/treaty-non-proliferation-nuclear-weapons>.

[50] Drawing on the observations in this chapter regarding the dynamic nature of treaty obligation, the present author intends to explore applying the Constructivist approach to understanding the nature of international legal norms and rules as well as the method of treaty interpretation. See discussion in Chaps. 6 and 7.

Chapter 4
The Afterlife of "Inalienable Right": Emergence of a New Regulatory Scheme in the Peaceful Use of Nuclear Energy

4.1 Introduction

Since the adoption of the Nuclear Nonproliferation Treaty, some new measures on nuclear controls have been introduced by the United States. The measures apply to the following three categories of activities/technologies: the so-called "sensitive" nuclear activities/technologies, dual-use activities/technologies, and conventional activities/technologies used in the nuclear industry. However, as is subsequently explained in this chapter, sensitiveness is a matter to be evaluated under different circumstances.

Nuclear activities/technologies, such as uranium enrichment, plutonium reprocessing, and heavy water manufacturing, have long been viewed as sensitive owing to their potential contribution to a country's nuclear capacity. However, after the NPT was entered into force, any proposed measures on the control of sensitive nuclear activities/technologies must be reviewed *de novo*. Indeed, control over sensitive nuclear activities became a source of dispute between the United States and Japan on Japan's indigenous nuclear recycling program, as well as between the United States and its European allies regarding nuclear exports. Supplier states also began to coordinate their policies on dual-use items and conventional nuclear items following the end of the Cold War. Many developing countries of the NPT States Party are averse to additional controls introduced beyond the IAEA-NPT framework, seeing them as excessive and an erosion of their right to the peaceful use of nuclear energy.

The United States believed that introducing all of these new measures was necessary because it found what it believed to be loopholes in the IAEA-NPT regulatory framework. To understand this argument, I first take an introductory note on the IAEA's role in the nuclear nonproliferation regime.

X. Zhang, *Law and Politics in Peaceful Use of Nuclear Energy*,
https://doi.org/10.1007/978-981-97-3813-7_4

4.2 IAEA and Peaceful Use of Nuclear Energy

International Atomic Energy Agency (IAEA) serves as the global focal point for decision-making and implementation related to facilitating international cooperation regarding the peaceful use of nuclear energy. The Agency engages mainly in three areas: Nuclear Safety and Security, Nuclear Science and Technology, and Safeguards and Verification.

The establishment of the Agency was a result of the U.S. nuclear policy transformation that occurred in the mid-1950s, when the United States abandoned a policy of strict denial of nuclear technology transfer and was about to seek a liberal regime for a world-wide cooperation in peaceful use of nuclear energy. However, this policy transformation was not unconditional: peaceful nuclear technology should not be diverted to military ends. This idea, promoted by United States President Dwight D. Eisenhower in his "Atoms for Peace" address to the General Assembly of the United Nations on December 8, 1953, also garnered endorsement from the Soviet Union despite nuclear rivalry at the time.

The two nuclear giants initiated the negotiation of the IAEA Statute immediately. In September 1956, the Conference for drafting the Statute of IAEA was convened at the United Nations headquarters in New York, though the UN served only as host rather than sponsor. On October 26, 1956, with the efforts made by the "Twelve Nations Group" whose members came from western and eastern blocs led by the United States and the U.S.S.R. respectively, the Statute was concluded and open for signature. The IAEA Statute entered into force on July 29, 1957. The IAEA headquarter and its Secretariat was set up in Vienna, Austria. The Agency grows over time to 178 member states as of 2023.

The IAEA is an independent intergovernmental organization in the United Nations family. However, it is not a Specialized Agency under Article 57 of the Charter of the United Nations. The relation of the IAEA with the United Nations is rather unique: it is independent from the United Nations but in the meantime, it maintains an even closer tie than the Specialized Agencies to the extent that the Agency has the right to submit reports and questions directly to the United Nations Security Council (IAEA Statute Article III, B, 4).

The IAEA consists of three statutory organs: The General Conference, the Board of Governors and the Secretariat. The General Conference comprises all member states while the Board of Governors, by setting up a complex membership requirements favors states with advanced nuclear technology. The Board of Governors is vested with broad authority to carry out the Agency's functions. In contrast, the General Conference is limited to requesting reports and making proposals on any matter relating to the functions of the Agency (IAEA Statute Article V.F.2). The Director General and staff shall work under the Board of Governors (IAEA Statute Article VII. B).

Through its various programs, the Agency promotes peaceful use of nuclear energy and prevents malicious applications of the technology. Developing countries are primarily interested in the assistance programs while the developed countries, particularly the United States and the U.S.S.R. following the 1962 Cuban missile crisis, sought to enhance measures in safeguarding peaceful nuclear activities from misuse. These dual mandates of cooperation and controls interact politically and concretely through financial and operational coordination, representing an ongoing balancing of perspectives.

The founders of the Agency designed the main field of the Agency's activities to be the assistance in many areas of nuclear research and application. The Statute initially proposed a rather modest nuclear safeguarding program: the Agency is only authorized to apply safeguards to what the Agency has supplied or assisted, or at the request of the member states (IAEA Statute Article III. A.5). However, the Treaty of Tlatelolco of 1967 and the Nuclear NonProliferation Treaty of 1968 all vested the Agency with the power of safeguarding nuclear activities in the States Party pursuant to the safeguards provisions in each treaty. Safeguards and Verification became a primary task of the Agency. The Agency's budget allocations over time evidenced such a functional evolution. The budget for Safeguards and Verification was only 3.4 percent of the regular budget in 1962 but grew to 24.1 percent by 1981 and reached UDS 102,278,000 in the year of 2004, exceeding the budget used in programs for Nuclear Safety and Security, plus Nuclear Science and Technology (USD 76,085,000).

The Board of Governors' original limited number and membership requirements (Article VI of the Statute) favored representation of developed states. As such, the Board was initially dominated by developed country voices, leading some to suggest this "rich nations' club" nature facilitated an evolving emphasis within the Agency away from assistance and toward safeguarding functions. However, amendments lifting the Board's membership cap over time from 23 to 35 have enabled greater developing state participation in decision-making processes.

Even as developing state representation within the Board of Governors increased over time, the IAEA Board of Governors continued strengthening the IAEA safeguards efforts aimed at detecting undeclared nuclear activities. For instance, in May 1997, a strengthened safeguards system, known as the Model Protocol Additional to IAEA Safeguards agreements (INFCIRC/540), was approved by the IAEA Board of Governors. It shows that the Agency's continual efforts in enhancing safeguards program have gained widespread support among both developed and developing IAEA member states alike.

In the field of Nuclear Safety and Security, the Agency codifies and publishes standards, guides and recommendations. Though not binding on member states, these international standards have substantial influence on national nuclear legislation governing radiation protection and nuclear reactor safety.

In addition to these activities, the Agency initiated and sponsored an impressive list of treaties to meet the need of international society in dealing with the international problems arising from the peaceful use of nuclear energy. These treaties cover subject matters such as liability of nuclear operations, early notification and assistance in nuclear accident, etc.

The IAEA has undoubtedly become an important institution in global governance due to its success over decades in delivering on the overarching objective established in its founding Statute—"to accelerate and enlarge the contribution of atomic energy to peace, health and prosperity throughout the world" (Article II). The IAEA continues working to both prevent malicious uses of these technologies and maximize safety, demonstrating an enduring commitment to its dual missions that has served the international community well and earned the organization's respected position it holds today.

4.3 Unilateralism in Regulating Sensitive Nuclear Activities/Technology

The IAEA functions in a way reflecting the spirit of multilateralism in the peaceful use of nuclear energy. Despite the apparent success of this important intergovernmental organization in promoting international cooperation in the field of the peaceful use of nuclear energy, the United States found some loopholes in the IAEA-NPT regulatory framework. This view appeared to underlie America's stance on selectively pursuing additional unilateral control initiatives, though others saw such moves as problematic.

The 1974 "peaceful nuclear explosion" conducted by India, which utilized assistance received from Canada (Deuterium Uranium Reactor (CANDU: CANDU-BLWR and CANDU-PHWR)) and the United States (heavy water) intended for its civilian nuclear programs—both subject to the IAEA-NPT safeguard system—served to validate American concerns about potential loopholes. Specifically, the CANDU-type reactor supplied by Canada was said to have contributed significantly to India's nuclear explosion.

Canada and the United States exhibited divergent approaches in addressing perceived shortcomings exposed by India's 1974 test. On the one hand, Canada still sought to work on the reliability of the NPT-IAEA regulatory system. Therefore, the new Canadian policy on nuclear exports focused on enhancing the safeguard measures.[1] On the other hand, the United States took the position that safeguard measures helped little in addressing the loopholes. From the United States' view, the assistance was deemed "sensitive" and, thus, warranted supplemental oversight beyond IAEA-NPT purview alone.

---

[1] The Canadian government, immediately after the Indian nuclear explosion, responded to the incident by announcing a restrained nuclear export policy but only to the extent of maximizing safeguards requirements. See "Announcement of Safeguards in Respect of Nuclear Material, Facilities and Technology by the Minister of Energy, Mines and Resources on 20th December 1974," reprinted in *The Regulation of Nuclear Trade*, Volume 2 National Regulations (Canada), (Nuclear Energy Agency OECD), p. 66.

4.3.1 The U.S. New Nonproliferation Policy on Sensitive Nuclear Activities/Technology

The notion of sensitive nuclear activity/technology emerged prominently through nonproliferation policies under the Ford and Carter Administrations in the 1970s. President Ford introduced controls on sensitive nuclear activities/technology in his 1976 Statement on United States Nuclear Policy, where he referenced sensitive areas like reprocessing and enrichment technology and facilities.[2] The new policy introduced measures such as postponing the U.S. domestic reprocessing program, banning sensitive nuclear exports, and calling on the other supplier countries to coordinate policy regarding sensitive exports.

The most explicit and comprehensive definition of "sensitive nuclear technology" can be found in the U.S. Atomic Energy Act amended in 1978 (also called Nuclear Non-Proliferation Act of 1978, hereafter the "1978 NNPA").[3] Sect. 4(a)(6) provides,

> "Sensitive nuclear technology" means any information (including information incorporated in a production or utilization facility or an important component part thereof) which is not available to the public and is important to the design, construction, fabrication, operation or maintenance of a uranium enrichment or nuclear fuel reprocessing facility or a facility for the production of heavy water.[4]

As defined in the 1978 NNPA legislation, the notion of sensitive nuclear activities/technologies encompasses technology, facilities, and materials in uranium enrichment, plutonium reprocessing, and heavy water manufacturing—all activities that are intrinsically closely connected to a state's ability to produce nuclear materials usable for nuclear weapons.

The precise definition of sensitive nuclear activity/technology was a late arrival in the Nuclear Nonproliferation Regime—it appears nowhere in the two basic legal documents of Nuclear Nonproliferation Regime—Statute of the International Atomic Agency and the Treaty on the Nonproliferation of Nuclear Weapons. As previously stated, this new nonproliferation policy on the control of sensitive nuclear activities/technologies was designed largely to address perceived loopholes in the NPT-IAEA system from the U.S. perspective. Since then, the same definition of sensitive nuclear activity/technology and corresponding measures have been extensively introduced in bilateral nuclear cooperation agreements between the United States and other countries.[5]

---

[2] "Ford Proposal on Nuclear Curbs Oct. 28, 1976," reprinted in *Historic Documents of 1976*, (Congressional Quarterly, Inc.), p. 830.

[3] "Nuclear Non-Proliferation Act (NNPA)," approved on March 10, 1978. *Public Law* 95–242.

[4] *Ibid.*

[5] Some examples can be found in Article 1(j) of the U.S.-Japan agreement; Article 9(f) of the Japan-Australia Agreement; Article 4(3) of Japan-Canadian protocol. See *Genshiryoku Kokusai Jyoyakushu (International Atomic Energy Agreements)* (Japan Atomic Industrial Forum, Inc. (JAIF) under supervision of Atomic Energy Bureau of Ministry of Foreign Affairs, 1994), p. 144, p. 245, p. 300.

In the U.S. new policies on nuclear nonproliferation, control over sensitive nuclear activities is primarily a matter of the U.S. national policy on nuclear exports. As President Ford announced, the United States Government would "have prohibited export of reprocessing and other nuclear technologies that could contribute to proliferation."[6] On another occasion, President Carter repeated the position that the United States will "continue to embargo the export of equipment or technology that would permit uranium and chemical reprocessing."[7] In both the Ford and Carter nuclear nonproliferation policies, U.S.-origin sensitive nuclear exports were no longer available even if such exports were subject to safeguards measures—the exports were prohibited unconditionally.

While tightening domestic controls on sensitive exports, the United States also pursued a supplemental nonproliferation approach internationally under this new policy. This included efforts to influence recipient states' indigenous nuclear fuel cycle (the case of Japan) and to interfere other supplier states' sensitive nuclear exports (the case of France and West Germany).

In nuclear power industry, the light water reactor (LWR) uses low-enriched uranium or MOX fuel that contains fissionable plutonium reprocessed from spent nuclear fuel. Therefore, to a certain extent, uranium enrichment and nuclear fuel reprocessing are indispensable to a country's indigenous nuclear power industry that uses light water reactors for power generation. Regarding Canadian CANDU–type reactors, although this type of reactor has become less popular in the nuclear power industry, it needs heavy water. Regarding uranium enrichment, nuclear fuel reprocessing, and heavy water, technologies have already been acquired by industrialized countries of the non-nuclear-weapon states (Western European states and Japan) through international cooperation with the United States, the United Kingdom, and France or independent efforts.[8] For these countries, uranium enrichment, plutonium reprocessing, and heavy water manufacturing have been legitimately part of peaceful nuclear energy applications.

Had the American policy been applied more strictly to its allied partners in Asia and Europe pursuing legitimate nuclear energy applications, it likely would have created significant political tensions. Japan in particular relied on indigenous fuel cycle capabilities. Western European states also competed in nuclear trade. However, the extent of any diplomatic fallout would have depended on how proportional and coordinated the new controls were in practice with America's key security and economic partners.

---

[6] *Supra* note 2, p. 827.

[7] "Carter Nuclear Policy, April 7, 27, 1977," reprinted in *Historic Documents of 1977* (Congressional Quarterly, Inc.), p. 271.

[8] See Sect. 2.3. of this study.

4.3.2 The New Policy and the Right of Prior Consent: The Case of U.S.–Japan Nuclear Energy Cooperation

Beyond restricting its own sensitive exports, American policy also envisioned exercising a degree of oversight over recipient states' nuclear programs by attaching conditions on its conventional nuclear exports. In such a case, the United States said that it would reserve its residual rights on the exported nuclear material and facilities—the rights were asserted as "prior consent rights" by the United States.

Prior consent rights appeared from time to time in bilateral nuclear cooperation agreements between the United States and recipient states. One example is the 1968 Agreement on Peaceful Use of Nuclear Energy between the United States and Japan. Paragraph C of Article 8 of the 1968 Agreement stipulated conditions such as "joint determinations" by both governments on sensitive downstream fuel cycle activities involving materials exported from America.[9] The "joint determination" had the practical effect of allowing the United States to retain a degree of oversight and authority over such proliferation-sensitive processes even when conducted within the recipient state's own facilities and territory, as was the case with reprocessing in Japan.

As the U.S. nonproliferation policy framed reprocessing abroad as proliferation-sensitive, the joint determination clause tied to Japan's first reprocessing facility built at Tokai Mura caused meaningful delays and uncertainty for Japan's indigenous fuel cycle plans. Considerable time elapsed before the two governments finally reached an agreement on jointly determining the conditional operation of the reprocessing facility at Tokai Mura, underscoring the challenges this conditionality created for a key ally pursuing what it viewed as legitimate nuclear energy applications.[10]

As the issue of "prior consent rights" took on greater strategic significance in American nonproliferation policy, their legal footing was strengthened through the 1978 NNPA legislation. By defining such conditionalities through an Act of Congress, it established "prior consent rights" as a statutory nonproliferation requirement for all of the United States' nuclear cooperation agreements going forward. This served to more formally and uniformly regulate a wider scope of American nuclear exports and extend oversight of downstream fuel cycle activities involving U.S.-origin materials and technology.[11]

---

[9] This is the "old agreement," concluded on July 10, 1968 and amended on December 21, 1973. See *supra* note 5.

[10] Shinsuke J. Sugiyama, "Peaceful Use of Nuclear Energy and the New Era for Japan-U.S. Cooperation-History and Major Issues of the New Japan-U.S. Agreement," *Japanese Annual of International Law,* Vol. 31(1988), pp. 20–21.

[11] Section 123 (a) (7) of the 1954 AEA as amended in Sect. 401 of 1978 NNPA, *Public Law* 95–242.

In the U.S.–Japan nuclear energy cooperation,[12] what troubled Japan in addition was the unilateral expansion of the prior consent rights to the so-called "derived material"—such as plutonium produced in U.S.-supplied light water reactors using non-U.S. origin low-enriched uranium. Given the U.S. supplied most of the low-enriched uranium and nuclear reactors throughout the world, enforcing this broad scope prior consent right risked subjecting most states' proliferation-sensitive programs to significant U.S. oversight, even when involving non-American origin materials and technologies.

While prior consent rights were established through bilateral nuclear cooperation agreements, the inherent asymmetry supplier-receiver structure limited the ability of the latter to meaningfully negotiate such conditionalities. In late 1970s and 1980s, the United States' interference into the Japanese indigenous fuel cycle through this mechanism became a significant diplomatic issue between these two countries.

In the dispute, Japan could rightly point to the "inalienable right" for peaceful uses of nuclear energy enshrined in the NPT, especially after it ratified the NPT in 1976. However, political prudence in maintaining ally's relation also factored significantly for a settlement. Ultimately, the new nuclear cooperation agreement between the two countries struck a balance by instituting a preferential programmatic approval arrangement for Japan, granting a long-term, predictable, and reliable basis for cooperation.[13] This programmatic approval is to be given on a one-time basis and will only be suspended under extreme circumstances—when the United States assesses proliferation risk threatening its national security is increasing.[14]

4.3.3 *Policy Coordination and the London Guidelines: Adjusting Trans-Atlantic Relations*

Apart from strict national controls over sensitive nuclear exports, the United States also called on the other supplier states to join it in exercising maximum restraint in sensitive nuclear exports. However, differences in the contents of sensitive nuclear

[12] Although Japan and the U.S. agreed in the "old" agreement of 1968 to let the agreement remain in force for a period of 35 years, a new agreement for cooperation was negotiated as a result of the enactment of the 1978 NNPA. Crucial issues included the "joint determination" and prior consent provisions. In the old Japan-U.S. agreement, "joint determination" did not cover uranium enrichment and "derived material." However, since uranium enrichment was developed using Japanese indigenous technology, including it under the "prior consent" terms in the new agreement troubled Japan less than "derived material." See *supra* note 5.

[13] See Article 11 of the new agreement and the implementing agreement. Similar arrangement was also made with Western European countries. See *supra* note 5.

[14] Shinsuke J. Sugiyama, *supra* note 10, p. 54. See also Imai Ryukichi, "Part 1, A Japanese View," in Imai Ryukichi and Henry S. Rowen, *Nuclear Energy and Nuclear Proliferation: Japanese and American Views* (Westview Press, 1980).

exports and the degree to which "restraint" should be exercised in controlling sensitive nuclear exports soon evolved into a major diplomatic confrontation in the mid-1970s. At that time, West Germany contracted with Brazil to supply its "sweetener" fuel recycling facilities in a package deal for its nuclear power station construction.[15] France had a deal with Pakistan regarding a fuel reprocessing facility.[16]

To stop such exports from the two countries, the United States adopted a stronger stance of urging maximum restraint.[17] The United States even threatened countermeasures if France and West Germany did not cancel such exportations. Senator Abraham Ribicoff once warned France and West Germany that if they did not stop, the United States would stop supplying nuclear fuel to the two countries.[18]

Ultimately, the two countries had to give in to the U.S. demand.[19] The compromise paved the way for more cooperative efforts—the establishment of an informal Nuclear Suppliers Group (NSG). The first international cooperation in controlling sensitive nuclear exports was made through a nonbinding multilateral agreement called the London Guidelines (London Guidelines Part One). These guidelines were initiated by the United States and agreed among members of the Nuclear Suppliers Group in September 1977. Article 7 of the Guidelines stipulates "special control on sensitive export," referring sensitive exports to enrichment or reprocessing facilities, equipment, or technology.[20] Members of the Group informally agreed that they would coordinate their sensitive nuclear exports, but stopped short of a full ban due to divergent viewpoints. Article 7 only required supplier states to exercise "restraint" in the transfer of sensitive facilities, equipment, or technology.[21] The ambiguity around "restraint" also allowed for independent supplier state interpretations.

In reconciling differences over the U.S. new policy, prudent diplomacy between the United States and its allies seemed to carry more weight than legal arguments alone. By offering "programmatic approval," the United States abstained from using its "prior consent rights" on its exports that may be used in sensitive Japanese nuclear activities, reducing Japan's insecurity regarding its long-term programs for the peaceful use of nuclear energy. France and West Germany set aside certain

[15] The cooperation agreement was made on June 27, 1975. On February 26, 1976, a tripartite safeguards agreement was made with IAEA. See IAEA Document, INFCIRC/237.

[16] A tripartite safeguards agreement was made with IAEA on March 18, 1976. See IAEA Document, INFCIRC/239.

[17] For example, President Ford "...call upon all nations to join us in exercising maximum restraint in the transfer of processing and enrichment technology and facilities by avoiding such sensitive exports or commitments for a period of at least three years." See "President Ford's Statement," reprinted in *Historic Documents of 1976* (Congressional Quarterly, Inc).

[18] Abraham A. Ribicoff, "Trading in Doom," *The New York Times,* Mar 26, 1976.

[19] Pierre Lellouche, "Breaking the Rule without Quite Stopping the Bomb: European Views," *International Organization,* Vol. 35 (1981), p. 47. (noting that France (December 16, 1976) and the West Germany (June 17, 1977) officially announced their policy on not exporting reprocessing facilities).

[20] "Guidelines for Nuclear Transfers in Communications received from certain Member States Regarding Guidelines for the Export of Nuclear Material, Equipment or Technology," IAEA Document, INFCIRC/254/Rev.1/Part 1, reprinted in *The International Law of Nuclear Energy,* 1517 seq.

[21] IAEA Document, INFCIRC/254.

deals and agreed to coordinate their policy on sensitive nuclear exports through the U.S.-initiated London Guidelines.

While the initial American policy understandably caused tensions as a unilateral action, it also spurred greater cooperation on developing multilateral controls. Nevertheless, international regulations on sensitive nuclear activities/technologies appears to be another form of unilateralism. This type of unilateralism aimed at separating sensitive nuclear activities from the general practice of the peaceful use of nuclear energy and put the former activities under more stringent control (rather than IAEA-NPT safeguards). At least from the perspective of the United States, a special tag has been successfully attached to sensitive nuclear activities—such activities are less "peaceful" when carried out by countries outside the Nuclear Suppliers Group.

4.4 Multilateralism Back and Forth

Understandably, the NPT States Party outside the Nuclear Suppliers Group questioned the legitimacy of this new international regulatory system on the ground that, as States Party, they clearly enjoy the "inalienable right" to the peaceful use of nuclear energy provided for in the NPT. Early American efforts acknowledged this tension and the need for inclusive dialogue to ensure all NPT members could pursue peaceful nuclear energy freely while curbing proliferation risks.

4.4.1 INFCE and the NSG-IAEA Cooperation

President Carter proposed the establishment of the International Nuclear Fuel Cycle Evolution (INFCE) as part of the Nuclear Nonproliferation Policy of his administration. The INFCE opening conference was held in Washington in October 1977, a month after members of the Nuclear Suppliers Group agreed on the London Guidelines Part One. INFCE was designed to offer some justification to the establishment of the Nuclear Suppliers Group and its Guidelines and to reduce hostility from developing countries toward the new regulatory system. However, INFCE's "technical findings" affirmed that under strengthened IAEA safeguards, all nations could pursue sensitive nuclear activities peacefully per their NPT rights—a perspective at odds with the U.S.[22]

Transparency and openness can help promoting legitimacy of nuclear control measures adopted by the Nuclear Suppliers Group. The London Guidelines was kept secret for a while after its adoption in 1977. However, the Nuclear Suppliers Group soon decided in 1978 to make it public. The Guidelines were later communicated to

[22] Victor Gilinsky, "Restraining the Spread of Nuclear Weapons: A Walk on the Supply Side," in Jed C. Snyder and Samuel F. Wells, Jr. eds. *Limiting Nuclear Proliferation* (Ballinger Publishing Company, 1985), pp. 264–265.

the IAEA, published as an IAEA document of INFCIRC/254. The publication of the Guidelines by IAEA indicated that Nuclear Suppliers Group was willing to be open and, thus, avoid the impression that the supplies were entering into a nuclear trading cartel.

4.4.2 Reinforcing Regulation: Controls on Dual-Use and Conventional Nuclear Items

In July 1991, Iraq admitted at the UN Security Council that it had been working on clandestine programs for uranium enrichment. The technology used in Iraqi clandestine uranium enrichments was a rather old method of electromagnetic separation of uranium (Calutron). Calutron technology was not covered by the London Guidelines Part One and was not treated as containing information "not available to the public" within the meaning of "sensitive nuclear technology" defined in Sect. 4 (a)(6) of the 1978 NNPA. The revelation of Iraq's covert enrichment program utilizing electromagnetic separation technology highlighted gaps in the initial control framework.

In the Second World War, calutron technology was used to produce high-enriched uranium in manufacturing atomic bombs. Enriching uranium using this method was energy-incentive and expensive. The calutron program in Oak Ridge (part of the Manhattan Project) is said to cost US$5 billion and consumed more electricity than what Canada produced during the entire Second World War.[23] Because of this, this technology has declassified since the end of the Second World War. The U.S. government never controlled the exports of specific calutron components.[24]

Given calutron technology's declassification after the Second World War, facilities, instruments, and technology that may help manufacture nuclear devices have been widely applied in non-nuclear industries. Iraq's pursuit of enrichment using publicly available calutron technology, along with advances enabling dual-use applications, revealed new loopholes in the existing control framework focused primarily on sensitive nuclear activities/technologies (U.S. domestic regulations and London Guidelines Part One). To close these new loopholes, the United States considered that the scope of sensitive nuclear activities may no longer be limited to activities associated with the nuclear fuel cycle. The scope of sensitive nuclear technology needed to be redefined to manage the new proliferation risk.[25]

It was suggested that sensitive nuclear technology should extend to cover equipment, materials, and technology that are not specially designed or prepared for the

---

[23] David Albright and Mark Hibbs, "Iraq's Nuclear Hide-and-seek," *Bulletin of the Atomic Scientists*, Vol. 47 (1991), p. 19.

[24] *Ibid.*, p. 18.

[25] John Simpson, "NPT Stronger after Iraq," *Bulletin of the Atomic Scientists*, Vol. 47 (1991), p. 13. (noting that the Nuclear Suppliers Group remained inactive from 1978 to the early 1990s before this new "loopholes" of NPT-IAEA system were exposed in Iraqi case).

nuclear energy industry (EDP items). For example, in the Iraqi calutron project, one key "sensitive" technology is the casting and rough machining of large iron components for the calutron project. These large iron components were made at Austrian and German foundries.[26] Another example is the Iraqi gas centrifuge project for uranium enrichment. A U.S. Senate hearing cited the IAEA finding that Du Pont was involved in supplying a vacuum pump oil that can be used in the Iraqi gas centrifuge project for uranium enrichment.[27] However, the lubricants were widely used in the electronics and chemical processing industries and Du Pont sold them to an Iraqi state-run company designed for oil production. In addition, the export received permission from the U.S. Government in 1989.[28]

The London Guidelines Part One did not cover the items that Iraq acquired through its clandestine uranium enrichment program. This became a major impetus for the Nuclear Suppliers Group to develop Dual-Use Guidelines published in March 1992 as the London Guidelines Part Two.[29] The Basic Principle of the Dual-Use Guidelines in Article 2 stipulated that exports would not be authorized in a situation "when there is an unacceptable risk of diversion to such an activity, or when the transfers are contrary to the objective of averting the proliferation of nuclear weapons." When implementing the Basic Principle in the export licensing process, factors such as "governmental actions, statements, and policies of the recipient state are supportive of nuclear nonproliferation" should also be taken into account (Article 4 (e)).

The Dual-Use Guidelines and Basic Principle on export controls on such dual-use items logically lead to reconsideration for further controls on conventional nuclear items, such as EDP items. New export controls may extend to nuclear power reactors—much depends on to whom they are exported. Under the London Guidelines Part One, nuclear reactors and other conventional EDP items were only subject to (later becoming full-scope) the safeguard regulation.[30] Nuclear power reactors never fell into sensitive nuclear exports controls.[31] However, if exports of both sensitive nuclear items and dual-use items require control measures in addition to safeguards, further controls will be required for exporting nuclear power reactors as well as other EDP items.

Nuclear Suppliers Group soon came to show its "proliferation concern" on conventional nuclear exports. In 1994, the Nuclear Suppliers Group adopted a "Nonproliferation Principle." According to this principle, NSG suppliers—notwithstanding other

---

[26] David Albright and Mark Hibbs, "Iraq's Shop-till-you-drop Nuclear Program," *Bulletin of the Atomic Scientists*, Vol. 48 (1992), p. 36.

[27] Congress, Senate, Committee on Foreign Relations, *Nuclear Proliferation: Learning from the Iraq Experience: Hearing before the Committee on Foreign Relations*, 102 Congress, October 17 and 23, 1991.

[28] "Du Pont Says U.S. Cleared Export of Items Used in Iraqi Bomb Effort," *The New York Times*, December 12, 1991.

[29] IAEA Document, INFCIRC 254/Part 2.

[30] "Trigger List Referred to in Guidelines" cover conventional nuclear items. They are subject to safeguards. See Article 4 of the London Guidelines Part1 (later modified as a full-safeguard requirement in the third NSG Conference).

[31] Article 7 and 8 of the London Guidelines Part1.

provisions in the NSG Guidelines—will not authorize transfers of sensitive nuclear items, conventional EDP items, and dual-use items unless they are satisfied that the transfer would not contribute to nuclear proliferation. By 1994, the NSG unified its control policy on sensitive, conventional, and dual-use items. On behalf of NSG member states, the Netherland Government explained this Nonproliferation Principle, "[the principle] seeks to cover the rare but important cases where adherence to the NPT or to a Nuclear Weapon Free Zone Treaty may not by itself be a guarantee that a States will consistently share the objectives of the Treaty or that it will remain in compliance with the Treaty obligation."[32]

The proposed sale of Russian power reactors to Iran served as an early case study in applying the newly adopted Nonproliferation Principle regarding exportation of conventional EDP items. Russia signed a nuclear cooperation agreement with Iran in January 1995.[33] Under the agreement, Russia would construct light water reactors for Iran's nuclear power plant at Bushehr. The first contracted reactor was to be completed within four years.[34]

The United States Government, attentive to nonproliferation priorities, opposed the proposed Russian reactor deal with Iran at a high diplomatic level. Specifically: (1) it provided to Iranian nuclear scientists and engineers through conventional reactor operation could develop a sophisticated understanding of nuclear technologies; (2)certain reactor materials and equipment may be at risk for unauthorized diversion; (3) Iran has the motivation to engage in a clandestine military nuclear program.[35] Additionally, because the final disposition of the spent fuel is not predetermined, it can be used by Iran in its secret reprocessing program.[36]

The Nuclear Suppliers Group's regulation on dual-use items and other conventional EDP items creates disparities between non-nuclear-weapon states within and outside Nuclear Suppliers Group. For example, as seen in the Russian–Iranian nuclear power plant deals, Iran—a party in good standing to the NPT—had difficulty acquiring even less proliferation-risky nuclear power plants from Russia. Meanwhile, similar light water reactors transferred under a U.S.-initiated Korean Peninsula Energy Development Organization (KEDO) initiative to replace North Korea's indigenous graphite reactors allegedly producing plutonium were not a nonproliferation concern. Indeed, the technological basis for KEDO recognized light water reactors posed a lower proliferation risk than other types. However, it remains uncertain

---

[32] IAEA Document, INFCIRC/539/Rev.1.

[33] "Iran, Russia Agree on $800 Million Nuclear Plant Deal," *The Washington Post*, January 9, 1995.

[34] "Iran's Nuke Plant Deal with Russia Fears," *The Washington Times*, January 10, 1995. David Albright and Mark Hibbs, "Nuclear Proliferation: Spotlight Shifts to Iran," *Bulletin of Atomic Scientists*, Vol. 48 (1992), p. 10 (noting that Iran also looked for nuclear cooperation from China). See also Steven Mufson, "Chinese Nuclear Officials See no Reason to Change Plans to Sell Reactors to Iran," *The Washington Post*, May18, 1995.

[35] Andrew Koch and Jeanette Wolf, "Iran's Nuclear Procurement Program: How Close to the Bomb?" *The Nonproliferation Review* Vol. 5 (Fall 1997), p. 128.

[36] *Ibid*., pp. 128–129.

whether target states of new export controls will consistently support nonproliferation treaty objectives and fulfill obligations.[37]

4.4.3 Response from Developing Countries of the NPT States Party

While historical disagreements surrounded interpretation of "inalienable right" and the scope of nonproliferation obligations,[38] developed countries were able to conclude multilateral nuclear controls agreements to coordinate their practice in this evolving nuclear nonproliferation regime. Non-nuclear-weapon states outside the Nuclear Suppliers Group reasonably inquire whether the NSG's controls respect their inalienable right to the peaceful use of nuclear energy under the NPT.

During the 1985 NPT Reviewing Conference, non-nuclear-weapon states not belonging to the NSG expressed perspectives regarding controls over sensitive nuclear activities.[39] While supplier states aimed for transparency, developing nations remained distrustful of unilateral measures. In reviewing Article IV of the NPT, the majority of the States Party viewed unilateral controls negatively. The Final Declaration on Article IV stated:

> …The Conference confirms that each country's choices and decisions in the field of peaceful uses of nuclear energy should be respected without jeopardizing their respective fuel-cycle policies...[40]

The information suggests the attitude of the developing States Party of the NPT toward nuclear controls began evolving following the end of the Cold War. This potential shift is meaningfully reflected in the pivotal 1995 NPT Review and Extension Conference.

In September 1994, the Non-Aligned Movement (NAM) and its supporters met in Indonesia to coordinate their stances prepared for the 1995 NPT Review and Extension Conference. In this meeting, participants agreed on a "Document on Substantive Issues Submitted by Indonesia on Behalf of the Group of Non-Aligned and Other States." The document criticized the "unjust restrictions and constraints" seen as impeding full access to nuclear technology, asserting "free and unimpeded access" under safeguards.[41]

In addressing the conference separately, Iran asserted that certain supplier states had contravened their Article IV obligations under the NPT relating to peaceful nuclear cooperation. Iran was quite clearly in a position that Article IV and the right to peaceful nuclear energy it enshrines should not be evaluated in connection with

---

[37] *Supra* note 32.

[38] See discussion in Sect. 5.2.

[39] The 1980 NPT Reviewing Conference failed to produce a Final Declaration.

[40] See U.N. Doc. NPT/CONF.III/64/I (September 21, 1985).

[41] Charles Van Doren, "Key NPT Conference Issues", *Arms Control Today*, Vol. 25 (1995), p. 19.

other provisions of the NPT.[42] For Iran, the right to the peaceful use of nuclear energy under Article IV is inalienable and absolute.

The 1995 NPT Review and Extension Conference presented an opportunity for developing states to clarify and reaffirm their peaceful nuclear rights, given parties were deciding the NPT's extension. This potential "bargaining chip" afforded leverage those countries previously lacked. However, discussions regarding Article IV and the rights it confers did not yield unexpected outcomes or influence the extension decision significantly. While some anticipated developing nations may push back on perceived inequities, consensus ultimately prevailed to strengthen the Treaty's long-term.[43]

While the 1995 Conference's Final Decision on Article IV reaffirmed the provision without substantive changes,[44] it did advocate for transparency in related exports through cooperative dialogue—"transparency in nuclear-related exports should be promoted within the framework of dialog and cooperation among all interested States party to the Treaty."[45] In response, NSG members agreed to establish a working group on transparency.[46]

4.5 Conclusion: A Double Separate and Unequal

International regulations on "sensitive nuclear activities" and growing multilateral controls on dual-use items and other conventional EDP items ultimately established an evolved regulatory framework for peaceful nuclear energy. The development of these expanded multilateral controls restructured the landscape of the global nuclear nonproliferation regime.

While the NPT divided the world into nuclear-weapon states and non-nuclear-weapon states, the development of multilateral nuclear controls helped delineate regulating states (Nuclear Supplier States and developed countries) and regulated states (Nuclear Recipient States and developing countries). Under this new regulatory scheme, while members of the Nuclear Suppliers Group faced fewer restrictions on certain operations, other NNWS parties encountered more limitations on peaceful nuclear imports depending on supplier views. After the Cold War ended, certain non-nuclear-weapon states became targets of "proliferation concerns" and their nuclear activities were further denied.

---

42 "NPT 'PrepCom' makes progress despite delays in final decision," *Arms Control Today*, Vol. 24 (1994), p. 21. For the discussion on the dispute between Iran and the U.S. in the NPT Preparatory Committee meeting for the 1995 NPT Review and Extension Conference in Geneva in September 1994, see Joseph F. Pilat and Charles W. Nakhleh, "A Treaty Reborn? The NPT After Extension," in Raju G. C. Thomas ed., *The Nuclear Non-proliferation Regime: Prospects for the 21st Century* (Macmillan Press, 1998), pp. 47–48.

43 Lewis A. Dunn, "High Noon for the NPT," *Arms Control Today*, Vol. 25 (1995), p. 8.

44 The 1995 NPT Review and Extension Conference 1995 Decision 2, paras. 14–16.

45 *Ibid.*, para. 17.

46 Available at <http://www.sipri.se/projects/amstrade/transparency_discussion.html>.

The NPT has long been regarded as unequal because it separates the haves from the have-nots. Now, the have-nots in the NPT seem to be further divided. Developed non-nuclear-weapon states may enjoy a broader "inalienable right" when they engage in sensitive nuclear activities. Developing non-nuclear-weapon states in the NPT are now subject to various regulations on their peaceful use of nuclear energy. This new distinction serves to exacerbate inequalities to some degree.

It is argued this new regulatory framework not only risks reducing trust from the non-nuclear-weapon states outside the NSG but also harms the nuclear nonproliferation regime over time. The example of Japan is presented as an NNWS party possessing sensitive facilities and technologies, with accumulated materials once rivaling some nuclear armed states' weapons stocks—suggesting capability to rapidly weaponize should a decision be made.[47]

Distrustful views held by some regulated states regarding multilateral controls reduce the prospects for such frameworks to be accepted as a subsequent practice that establishes "the agreement of the parties" concerning the "interpretation" of the "inalienable right" and the relevant NPT provisions. The gap between NSG members and nonmembers in interpreting "inalienable right" remains huge.

---

[47] Atsushi Tsuchida, "The Nuclear Arming of Japan," in William M Evan and Ved P. Nanda eds., *Nuclear Proliferation and the Legality of Nuclear Weapons* (University Press of America, 1995), pp. 99–115. (noting that Japan has never given up the nuclear option. Japan's position has been that it will not go nuclear as long as the U.S. nuclear umbrella remains applicable to its defense. However, Japan's accumulation of large stockpiles of plutonium has consistently faced scrutiny from a nonproliferation perspective. Some analysts have even warned that Japan's production of high-purity plutonium by using its breeder project represents a tangible step towards developing tactical nuclear weapons).

Chapter 5
Intentional Ambiguity and the Rule of Interpretation in the Autointerpretation of "Inalienable Right" in the NPT Article IV

5.1 Introduction

The 1968 Treaty on the Nonproliferation of Nuclear Weapons contains provisions employing indeterminate language, such as the term "manufacture" in Articles I and II of the NPT,[1] the terms "inalienable right" and "right to participate" in Article IV, and "obligation" that a State Party "undertakes to pursue negotiations in good faith on effective measures relating to cessation of the nuclear arms race at an early date and to nuclear disarmament" in Article VI. The terms "manufacture" in Articles I and II and "inalienable right" in the first paragraph of Article IV are interrelated, indicating real ambiguity about the scope of prohibition on manufacture as well as the extent of the inalienable right that States Party enjoy. This lack of definitional clarity in "real ambiguity" provisions, as exemplified by ongoing legal debates about the Iranian nuclear problem, tends to give rise to interpretive disputes. By contrast, the "right to participate" in the second paragraph of Article IV and the "obligation" to pursue good faith negotiations in Article VI are hortatory or inspirational in nature. They are merely "contracts to contract,"[2] and subject to further consensus in subsequent negotiations. As far as ambiguity in application of certain provisions using hortatory or aspirational language in founding documents will be dispelled through subsequent negotiations, such hortatory clauses may not present significant difficulties in interpretation going forward.

The most straightforward way towards clarifing the ambiguous scope of the "inalienable right" is perhaps treaty modification.[3] However, it is "unrealistic," not

---

[1] Eric Stein, "Legal Restraints in Modern Arms Control Agreements," *American Journal of International Law*, Vol. 66 (1972), pp. 276–277.

[2] D. W. Greig, "The Interpretation of Treaties and Article IV.2 of the Nuclear Non-Proliferation Treaty," *Australian Year Book of International Law*, Vol. 6 (1974–1975), p. 101.

[3] For the NPT as a whole, see Rein Mullerson, "The ABM Treaty: Changed Circumstances, Extraordinary Events, Supreme Interests and International Law," *International and Comparative Law Quarterly*, Vol. 50 (2001), p. 529. For "inalienable right" in sensitive activities, Ryukichi Imai once

X. Zhang, *Law and Politics in Peaceful Use of Nuclear Energy*,
https://doi.org/10.1007/978-981-97-3813-7_5

only because developing countries would oppose such modification, but also because a formal amendment to the NPT would open a diplomatic Pandora's Box.[4] While States Party may avoid amendment procedures if they can reach consensus on the interpretation of a treaty provision,[5] debate remains on legal techniques that will be employed to clarify the ambiguous text.[6]

This Chapter focuses on the interpretative problem of "inalienable right." It is desirable to settle the problem by "authoritative interpretations" rendered by treaty-based institutional organs (e.g., an authorized committee established by the treaty, COP/MOP decisions or resolutions by Review Conferences) or by a third party judicial process. However, these methods may be impractical, due to the highly political nature of the issue.[7] They may likely be ineffective, as consensus outcomes from review processes risk compromising definitional clarity by reiterating ambiguous language.[8] Therefore, absent a competent institutional organ which is capable of rendering universally binding interpretations, an initial decentralized approach respecting each state's role in equal auto-interpretation settles conflicts between norms and their interpretation.[9]

When assessing autointerpretation, criteria like the "general rule of interpretation" codified in Article 31 as well as the "supplementary means of interpretation"

---

suggested not to outlaw sensitive activities as a whole, but to use a "more discriminatory approach." He proposed to separate the "unqualified states" from the "qualified states" through treaty modification to settle the problem concerning "inalienable right." See Ryukichi Imai and Henry S. Rowen, *Nuclear Energy and Nuclear Proliferation: Japanese and American Views* (Westview Press,1980), p. 45, p. 72, p. 167. In the same vein on the indeterminate language of Articles 1, 3 and 5 of the BWC, Beard suggested a draft protocol to prescribe the control list. See Jack M. Beard, "The Shortcomings of Indeterminacy in Arms Control Regimes: The Case of the Biological Weapons Convention," *American Journal of International Law*, Vol. 101 (2007), p. 314.

4 Joseph Nye, "New Approach to Nuclear Proliferation Policy," *Science*, Vol. 256 (1992), p. 295.

5 Burrus M. Carnahan and Katherine L. Starr, "Law and Policy in the Amendment of Arms Control Agreements," *Loyola of Los Angeles International and Comparative Law Review*, Vol. 20 (1997—1998), p. 632.

6 When the treaty provision is clear, there seems to be a line between modification and interpretation. An "interpretation" to render a different meaning is indeed modification and therefore not permissible. The International Law Commission in its commentary on the 1966 draft cited *The Interpretation of Peace Treaties (Advisory Opinion)* to show that "(the court) emphasized that to adopt an interpretation which ran counter to the clear meaning of the terms would not be to interpret but to revise the treaty." Also, the Court in the *U.S. Nationals in Morocco* case stated that "the court has more than once stressed that it is not the function of interpretation to revise or read into them what they do not expressly or by implication, contain." Therefore, when commenting on Article 38 of the 1966 Draft, the ILC further elaborated that: "Although the line may sometimes be blurred between interpretation and amendment of a treaty through subsequent practice, legally the processes are distinct." See *Yearbook of the International Law Commission* 1966 Vol. II, pp. 219–221, p. 236.

7 Eric Stein, supra note 1, pp. 274–275, Ian Johnstone, "Treaty Interpretation: The Authority of Interpretive Communities," *Michigan Journal of International Law*, Vol. 12 (1990—1991), p. 372.

8 The "inalienable right" of the NPT States Party in peaceful application of nuclear energy has been "affirmed" on various occasions. See infra notes 66–69 and accompanying text.

9 Dinah Shelton, "Reconcilable Differences: The Interpretation of Multilingual Treaties," *Hastings International and Comparative Law Review*, Vol. 20 (1996–1997), p. 322. On autointerpretation in the context of Article IV of the NPT, see D. W. Greig, *supra* note 2, p. 81.

in Article 32 of the Vienna Convention on the Law of Treaties, provide legal benchmarks, as States are bound by the said rules in making autointerpretation.[10]

This chapter provides contextual background to the issue of interpretation in Article IV of the NPT by briefly reviewing the arguments relevant to the events triggered by shifts in U.S. nuclear policy. It notes the "inalienable right" poses greater ambiguity than the "right to participate" in defining permissible activities. The chapter examines various autointerpretations concerning the "inalienable right," particularly relating to North Korea and Iran, with initial reference to the general rule of interpretation under Article 31 of the Vienna Convention on the Law of Treaties. The primary aims are to analyze challenges in construing the "inalienable right" and identify limitations in practically applying the general rule of interpretation.

5.2 The Issue Concerning Interpretation of Article IV of the NPT

Article IV of the NPT stipulates as follows:

1. Nothing in this Treaty shall be interpreted as affecting the inalienable right of all the Parties to the Treaty to develop research, production and use of nuclear energy for peaceful purposes without discrimination and in conformity with Articles I and II of this Treaty.
2. All the Parties to the Treaty undertake to facilitate, and have the right to participate in, the fullest possible exchange of equipment, materials and scientific and technological information for the peaceful uses of nuclear energy. Parties to the Treaty in a position to do so shall also co-operate in contributing alone or together with other States or international organizations to the further development of the applications of nuclear energy for peaceful purposes, especially in the territories of non-nuclear-weapon States Party to the Treaty, with due consideration for the needs of the developing areas of the world.[11]

Subsequent events occurred in connection with shifts in U.S. policy from the mid-1970s aimed at exerting increased oversight on sensitive nuclear activities. While the term "sensitive nuclear activity" appears nowhere in the two basic legal documents of

---

[10] However, nuance exists between the general rule of interpretation of Article 31 and the supplementary means of interpretation of Article 32. While Article 31 explicitly stipulates "shall" and thus is obligatory, Article 32 "may" only be used when the text is ambiguous or when the general rule of interpretation produce absurd results, indicating the nature of the conditional and discretional "means." The general rule of interpretation has been confirmed as customary law by the ICJ. See *Territorial Dispute (Libya v. Chad)*, I.C.J. Reports 1994, p. 19, para. 41. For an overall discussion on the codification of pre-existing customary law in Articles 31–33, see Evan Criddle, "The Vienna Convention on the Law of Treaties in U.S. Treaty Interpretation," *Virginia Journal of International Law*, Vol. 44 (2003–2004), pp. 445–448.

[11] Treaty on the Nonproliferation of Nuclear Weapons, opened for signature July 1, 1968, entered into force March 5, 1970, extended indefinitely in the 1995 NPT Review and Extension Conference), 729 UNTS 161. Article IV.

the nuclear non-proliferation regime, namely, the Statute of the International Atomic Agency and the NPT, it refers to nuclear activities sensitive to proliferation, and encompasses reprocessing, enrichment and heavy water technologies and facilities.[12]

This new policy on controlling sensitive activities, had it been fully implemented, could have effectively banned sensitive nuclear exports, disrupting fuel-importing countries' indigenous fuel cycles as well as interfering with other supplier States' sensitive nuclear exports. This policy shift prompted two lines of interpretive argument regarding Article IV. First, debates emerged around how export controls aligned with Article IV's stipulation of the "right to participate" in the fullest possible exchange of equipment, materials and scientific and technological information for the peaceful uses of nuclear energy. Second, questions arose over whether indigenous sensitive nuclear activities fell within the scope of states' "inalienable right," or if certain activities could be excluded.

On the question of "right to participate," the core issue concerns whether this encompasses the right of supplier and/or recipient states to undertake sensitive nuclear export/import activities. Moreover, if recipient States have the right to acquire sensitive nuclear technologies, does this infer a legal obligation on the part of the countries that are in the position to supply such technologies to make such supply? This question emerged as a point of debate in trans-Atlantic disputes between the U.S. and European countries in the second half of the 1970s, when Germany prepared sensitive nuclear exports to Brazil, and France to Pakistan and South Korea.

From the supplier perspective, a West German spokesman justified the German-Brazil reprocessing export by stating "Germany is simply following the provisions of Article IV of the NPT, which binds subscribers to facilitate the fullest possible exchange of equipment, materials and scientific and technological information for the peaceful uses of nuclear energy…with due consideration for the needs of the developing areas of the world."[13] Bertrand Goldschmidt, a former chairman of the Board of Governors of the IAEA, similarly agreed that restrictions on the transmission of sensitive technologies can be construed as a breach of "the *promise* set forth in Article IV of the NPT."[14] (emphasis added). However, the perspective of recipient countries on whether their "right to participate" had been infringed by the change in supplier states export policy was not included in discussions at that time[15] when

[12] For the U.S. policy and law, see "Ford Proposal on Nuclear Curbs Oct. 28, 1976," reprinted in *Historic Documents of 1976*, (Congressional Quarterly, Inc.), p. 830; Sect. 4 (a)(6) of "Nuclear Non-Proliferation Act (NNPA)," approved on March 10, 1978. Public Law 95–242. For bilateral nuclear cooperation agreements, see Article 1(j) of the U.S.-Japan agreement; Article 9(f) of the Japan-Australia Agreement; Article 4(3) of Japan-Canadian protocol. *Genshiryoku Kokusai Jyoyakushu [International Atomic Energy Agreements]* (Japan Atomic Industrial Forum, Inc. (JAIF) under supervision of Atomic Energy Bureau of Ministry of Foreign Affairs, 1994), p. 144, p. 245, p. 300.

[13] William W. Lowrance, "Nuclear Future for Sale: To Brazil from West Germany, 1975," *International Security*, Vol. 1 (1976), p. 154.

[14] Bertrand Goldschmidt, "A Historical Survey of Nonproliferation Policies," *International Security* Vol. 2 (19 77), p. 80.

[15] Brazil became a State Party to the NPT in the year of 1998 and Pakistan remained outside the NPT. South Korea became a State Party to the NPT on 23 April 1975 but remained silent on this issue.

sensitive technology transfer deals were cancelled due to pressure exerted by the U.S. on suppliers and/or recipients.[16]

It seems that the suppliers' "right to participate" as described in paragraph 2 of Article IV, even established, remains subject to the discretion of supplier States. After all, it is the "right" of the suppliers and therefore it is up to them to decide whether or not, and in what manner, they will implement such a right. It is in this sense that Mr. Charles N. Van Doren argued for multilateral nuclear export controls: "Supplier States will certainly not agree that Article IV eliminates their sovereign right to choose their trading partners or compels them to suspend judgment on whether certain requested nuclear exports to some States are inconsistent with the primary objective of the NPT as set forth in Articles I and II."[17] As a matter of fact, this kind of discretion has been collectively formalized by the non-binding London Guidelines, requiring suppliers to take "special controls on sensitive exports."[18]

Recipient States' "right to participate" in Article IV would require corresponding obligations on the suppliers who are in a position to provide assess: "the vital issues are whether this sentence creates a legal obligation; and if it does, what is the extent of the obligation."[19] However, the travaux préparatoires of Article IV of the NPT indicates a proposed imposition of a "duty" or "judicial commitment" on the supplier States was rejected.[20] At most, any implied obligation remains incomplete or "a contract to make a contract."[21] The language overall is characterized as hortatory.[22] Rather than a matter of interpretation, the challenge involves reconciling suppliers'

[16] For example, Senator Abraham Ribicoff warned France and West Germany that if they did not stop these sensitive exports, the U.S. would stop supplying nuclear fuel to these two counties. See Abraham A. Ribicoff, "Trading in Doom," *The New York Times*, Mar 26, 1976. As a result, the two supplier countries bent to the U.S. pressure, see Pierre Lellouche, "Breaking the Rule without Quite Stopping the Bomb: European Views," *International Organization*, Vol. 35 (1981), p. 47. (noting France (December 16, 1976) and the West Germany (June 17, 1977) officially announced their policy on not exporting reprocessing facilities.) Thomas L. Neff and Henry D. Jacoby, "Nonproliferation Strategy in a Changing Nuclear Fuel Market," *Foreign Affairs*, Vol. 57 (1978–1979), p. 1127. (noting that South Korea gave up the plan to purchase a reprocessing plant from France under the U.S. pressure).

[17] Charles Van Doren, "Key NPT Conference Issues," *Arms Control Today*, Vol. 25 (1995), p. 19. Mr. Doren is the former Assistant Director of the Arms Control and Disarmament Agency for Non-Proliferation and served as the U.S. alternative representative to the 1975 and 1980 NPT Review Conferences.

[18] Referring sensitive exports to enrichment or reprocessing facilities, equipment, or technology. Guidelines for Nuclear Transfers in Communications received from certain Member States Regarding Guidelines for the Export of Nuclear Material, Equipment or Technology, INFCIRC/254/Rev.1/Part 1, reprinted in, *The International Law of Nuclear Energy*, p. 1517 seq.

[19] D. W. Greig, *supra* note 2, p. 89.

[20] Edwin Brown Firmage, "The Treaty on the Non-Proliferation of Nuclear Weapons," *American Journal of International Law*, Vol. 63 (1969), p. 728. See also discussion at Sect. 3.3.2 of this study.

[21] D. W. Greig, *supra* note 2, p. 101.

[22] Edwin Brown Firmage, *supra* note 20, p. 728. See also discussion at Sect. 3.3.2 of this study.

"duty to negotiate subsequent arrangements in good faith,"[23] with the discretion that they retain in implementing their own right to participate.

The core interpretive issue remaining to be resolved concerns the scope of "inalienable right" referenced in Article IV, paragraph 1. The interpretation issue here is specific: should domestic sensitive nuclear activities be excluded from the "inalienable right" of all signatories to participate in nuclear activities? The relevance of the qualifying phrase "in conformity with Articles I and II of this Treaty" adds complexity, as a literal reading could exclude manufacturing activities prohibited under those Articles. Particularly regarding non-nuclear-weapon State Parties, Article II stipulates certain restrictions:

> Each non-nuclear-weapon State Party to the Treaty undertakes not to receive the transfer from any transferor whatsoever of nuclear weapons or other nuclear explosive devices or of control over such weapons or explosive devices directly, or indirectly; not to manufacture or otherwise acquire nuclear weapons or other nuclear explosive devices; and not to seek or receive any assistance in the manufacture of nuclear weapons or other nuclear explosive devices.[24] (emphasis added).

The immediate disagreement arose from U.S.'s Western European allies and Japan in the late 1970s and early 1980s, as non-nuclear-weapon States Party to the NPT with capacities and interests in the sensitive fields of the civilian nuclear industry. The United States government justified the U.S. new nuclear nonproliferation policy controlling sensitive nuclear activities by asserting the inalienable right must be subject to the condition of "in conformity with Articles I and II of this Treaty." For instance, the U.S. representative in the First Committee of UN General Assembly stated, "We have continued to fulfill our commitments under the NPT Article IV …with the restraints required by Articles I and II."[25]

West Germany and Japan were two major states dissenting from the new U.S. nuclear nonproliferation policy in late 1970s. However, the new U.S. policy was not intended to specifically target these developed countries.[26] It has never been fully implemented for such countries, instead applied selectively to some developing countries.[27] The effects of this selective approach in U.S. non-proliferation policy can be seen today in nuclear issues facing the Korean peninsula and Iran, with both situations reviving interpretation differences.

---

[23] It is very much similar to Article VI of the NPT, which is also regarded as a problem of implementation. See Edwin Brown Firmage, *supra* note 20, p. 746.

[24] Treaty on the Nonproliferation of Nuclear Weapons, *supra* note 11, Article II.

[25] U.N. Doc. A/C.1/31/PV.20/37.

[26] Thomas L. Neff and Henry D. Jacoby, *supra* note 16, p. 1132.

[27] Richard Falk commented on the outcome of the selective implementation of the new U.S. nonproliferation policy as "virtually no notice" to Japanese and German acquisition of the technical capabilities to support a possible future mid-scale nuclear weapons program. See Richard Falk, "The Illegitimacy of the Non-Proliferation Regime," *Brown Journal of World Affairs*, Vol. 4 (1997), pp. 73–74.

The upcoming discussion will analyze trends in autointerpretation of the NPT treaty clauses over time. Particular attention will be paid to how changing circumstances and policy have impacted such auto-interpretations, and the degree to which different interpretations have relied upon established rules of interpretation.

5.3 Autointerpretations on "Inalienable Right" and Their *Prima Facie* Reliance on Article 31 of the VCLT: The Past and the Present

It is true that the text of paragraph 1 of Article IV prescribes that non-nuclear-weapon States Party's exercise of the "inalienable right" must conform with Articles I and II. But what precisely constitutes the prohibited activities of "manufacture" requiring exclusion from the "inalienable right"?

5.3.1 Restrictive Interpretation of Ambiguous Text

The Japanese Government, upon signing the NPT in 1970, issued a statement asserting Japan's lack of intent to build weapons should not preclude other peaceful technological options, even if containing proliferation risks.[28] This perspective was echoed by a German diplomat on another occasion.[29] Such an interpretation implies a broad conception of the "inalienable right," with a comparatively narrow scope of manufacturing activities deemed necessary to ban.

This kind of interpretation has been widely accepted among non-proliferation experts. For example, F. Barnaby at the Stockholm International Peace Research Institute ("SIPRI") pointed out that preparatory manufacturing actions close to weaponry did not necessarily constitute the banned activities in Article II. He wrote: "A party to the NPT could legally manufacture the components of any number of nuclear weapons, and the non-nuclear parts of the weapons could be assembled. Only when the fissile material was placed into one of the devices would the Treaty be broken."[30]

---

[28] U.S. Arms Control and Disarmament Agency Document on Disarmament (1969), pp. 609–611; U.S. Arms Control and Disarmament Agency Document on Disarmament (1970), pp. 2–5.

[29] Werner Ungerer (German Consul General)'s speech at a symposium (1977), cited in Ian Johnstone, *supra* note 7, pp. 411–412.

[30] Cited in R. Jorn S. Harry, "IAEA Safeguards and Non-proliferation," in Marianne van Leeuwn (ed.), *The Future of the International Nuclear Non-proliferation Regime* (Martinus Nijhoff Publishers, 1995), p. 170, at note 7.

Bertrand Goldschmidt similarly summarized the NPT policy as prohibiting explosion allowing other pursuits, with nothing preventing States Party from following the technical path of their choice.[31]

This interpretation would naturally conclude that any part of the fuel cycle, including sensitive activities, should not constitute the banned "manufacturing" activities under Article II, and therefore must remain within States' "inalienable right." Goldschmidt noted, "...it is unfortunate that the danger, from a proliferation point of view, of the enrichment and reprocessing step is nowhere reflected in the NPT which in [A]rticle IV underlines the right of access to the civilian fuel cycle for all member countries...".[32] Similarly, Pierre Lellouche argued from a European perspective, that these changes (restrictions on the "inalienable right" by tabooing sensitive nuclear activities) were seen as attempts to rewrite valid international norms and agreement.[33] For Lellouche, Article IV established the "normal rule of the time" as a guarantee for non-nuclear weapon States Party of access to the entire fuel cycle.[34] Japanese experts shared their European colleagues' interpretations of the "inalienable right." Ryukichi Imai criticized the new U.S. nonproliferation policy in 1978 which restricted sensitive nuclear activities: "...what bothers me is the manner in which the U.S. version of the truth is forcefully presented to the world, including unilateral changes in multilateral accords such as the Nuclear Nonproliferation Treaty."[35] Imai believed "international community cannot tolerate the imposition of a unilateral shift in what is basically a multilateral accord."[36] A decade later, Shinsuke J. Sugiyama, a Japanese diplomat negotiating the 1988 Japan-U.S. Agreement for Cooperation on Peaceful Use of Nuclear Energy, also articulated this view, subtly suggesting the U.S. policy interfering with Japan's reprocessing project "signified an ideological deviation from the NPT principles."[37]

Ironically, this view on the relation between sensitive activities and the scope of the "inalienable right" was also the position of the U.S. government before it undertook policy shift in the mid-1970s. In the U.S. Senate consent hearing on the NPT,[38] the Director of the U.S. Arms Control and Disarmament Agency (ACDA) explicitly excluded uranium enrichment, storage of fissile material, power reactors fueled with plutonium, fast breeder reactors, and other activities from Article II's prohibition, so

---

[31] Bertrand Goldschmidt, *Nuclear Non-proliferation and Safeguards, A Conference Report* (The Atlantic Institute for International Affairs, The American Nuclear Society, 1981), p. 66.

[32] Bertrand Goldschmidt, *supra* note 14, p. 80. (noting that these restrictions on the transmission of sensitive technologies can be construed as a breach of the promise given in Article IV of the NPT).

[33] Pierre Lellouche, *supra* note 16, p. 45.

[34] *Ibid.*, p. 45.

[35] Ryukichi Imai, "A Japanese Reaction to U.S. Nonproliferation Policy," *International Security*, Vol. 3 (1978), p. 62.

[36] Ryukichi Imai and Henry S. Rowen, *supra* note 3, p. 75.

[37] Shinsuke J. Sugiyama, "Peaceful Use of Nuclear Energy and the New Era for Japan-U.S. Cooperation-History and Major Issues of the New Japan-U.S. Agreement," *Japanese Annual of International Law*, Vol. 31 (1988), p. 20.

[38] See U.S. Constitution, Art. II, § 2, which requires the Senate's "consent" of international treaties.

long as adequate safeguarded prevented abuse.[39] Nevertheless, nowadays the U.S. government tends not to address this issue in its official statements on Article IV of the NPT.[40]

Most recently, North Korea and Iran faced international pressure when conducting sensitive nuclear activities. However, sanctions and legal arguments centered more on North Korea's violations of the NPT safeguards and the withdrawal clause.[41] While North Korea did not assert a substantive right under the NPT to develop reprocessing or enrichment technologies,[42] Iran on various occasions defended its nuclear program and enrichment as falling under the "inalienable right" of paragraph 1 of Article IV.[43]

As for the legality of sensitive activities in North Korea and Iran, most U.S. non-proliferation experts would have relied upon the traditional interpretation when referring to ambiguous treaty texts.[44] Natasha Bajema and Mary Beth Nikitin restated "the NPT allows the development of proliferation-sensitive technology such as uranium enrichment and spent fuel reprocessing and does not prohibit the stockpiling of

---

[39] Statement by ACDA Director Foster on the Non-proliferation Treaty, Foreign Relations Committee, Senate, July 10, 1968. Treaty interpretation in the U.S. may be informed by explanations provided to the U.S. Senate during the ratification process. The U.S. Constitution requires the Senate's "advice and consent" for international agreements (Art. II, § 2). See A. Rubin, "The Theology of Arms Control and U.S. Politics," *The Christian Science Monitor*, June 2, 1987, p. 16.

[40] U.S. Department of State, Article IV of the NPT: U.S. Support for Peaceful Nuclear Cooperation, Fact Sheet, Bureau of Non-Proliferation (Jan. 20, 2001), available at <https://2001-2009.state.gov/t/isn/rls/fs/2001/3052.htm>.

[41] For more discussions on North Korean safeguards violations and problems in the withdrawal clause, see Masahiko Asada, "Arms Control Law in Crisis-A Study of the North Korean Nuclear Issue," *Journal of Conflict and Security Law*. Vol. 9, (2004) p. 331 seq.; Maurice Andem, "The Treaty on the Non-Proliferation of Nuclear Weapons (NPT)-Some Reflections in the Light of North Korea's Refusal to Allow International Inspection of Its Nuclear Facilities," *Nordic Journal of International Law*, Vol. 64 (1995), p. 587. As to Iran, the UNSC resolutions on the Iranian nuclear issue (Res.1696, 1737 and 1747) were all based on safeguards violations. See Jack M. Beard, *supra* note 3, pp. 317–318; Arsalan M. Suleman, "Bargaining in the Shadow of Violence: The NPT, IAEA, and Nuclear Non-Proliferation Negotiations," *Berkeley Journal of International Law*, Vol. 26 (2008), pp. 237–238.

[42] *Ibid.*, Arsalan M. Suleman, p. 235.

[43] Foreign Minister of Iran Defends Country's Inalienable Right to Nuclear Technology for Peaceful Purposes (Jan. 29, 2004), available at <https://www.un.org/press/en/2004/dcf433.doc.htm>.

[44] There may be only one exception in Maurice Andem's 1995 article on North Korea, in which he claimed that prohibitions in Article II are very clear and explicit, and "any activity or process carried out by them (non-nuclear-weapon States) with the aim of producing any type of material necessary for the manufacture of nuclear weapons, is contrary to the provisions of the NPT and therefore illegal under contemporary international law." See Maurice Andem, *supra* note 41, p. 584. However, the present author notes that Andem provides no explanation for stating these prohibitions are "clear and explicit."

weapon-grade nuclear material...".[45]David Sloss similarly concluded that a non-nuclear-weapon State Party to the NPT could acquire a legal stockpile of weapons-grade nuclear material under the IAEA safeguards, though he did fear that these countries may subsequently announce their withdrawal from the NPT, and then proceed to manufacture nuclear weapons.[46]

Indeed, disputes referred to the UN Security Council involve non-compliance with the safeguards agreements, not rights-based claims.[47] While the UN Security Council may mandate sanctions under Chap. 7 of the UN Charter for "threat to the peace," these are not necessarily imposed due to violations of the NPT provisions. As Suleman correctly pointed out, sanctions on Iranian enrichment activities were not based on the proposition that these activities were illegal under the NPT, but on Iran's past safeguards noncompliance. Therefore, it gave UN Security Council grounds to declare Iran's current enrichment activities a threat to international peace and security, thereby providing legal recourse to impose sanctions.[48]

If solely considering the ambiguous text of Article II and Article IV, the majority opinion would be sensitive nuclear activities conducted as part of the fuel cycle fall outside the scope of prohibited "manufacture" and within the "inalienable right". This "textual" interpretation aligns with the principle of restrictive interpretation of sovereignty—"a convention [treaty] is not intended to restrict State sovereignty to a degree beyond what is *explicitly stated in its provisions*."[49] (emphasis added). For non-nuclear-weapon states under the NPT, sovereignty inherently includes rights beyond solely weapon possession. Their other rights were retained and reaffirmed as the "inalienable right" to develop, research, and use nuclear energy "without discrimination" for peaceful purposes.[50]

---

[45] Natasha Bajema and Mary Beth Nikitin, "Assessing Nuclear Maturity: Determining Which States Should Have Access to What Nuclear Technology," *Fletcher Forum of World Affairs*, Vol. 28 (2004), p. 159.

[46] David Sloss, "Forcible Arms Control: Preemptive Attacks on Nuclear Facilities," *Chicago Journal of International Law*, Vol. 4 (2003), p. 40.

[47] Arsalan M. Suleman, *supra* note 41, p. 224.

[48] *Ibid*., p. 239.

[49] Opinion of M. Susterhenn, Wemhoff v. The Federal Republic of Germany, Report of the Commission, Document 2771 06.2/31, p. 86, cited in Clovis C. Morrisson, Jr., "Restrictive Interpretation of Sovereignty-Limiting Treaties: The Practice of the European Human Rights Convention System," *International and Comparative Law Quarterly*, Vol. 19 (1970), p. 370. On the restrictive interpretation, see also Robert Y. Jennings and Sir Arthur Watts, *Oppenheim's International Law*, Vol. I (9th ed. Longman, 1992), p. 1278; Gillian White, "Treaty Interpretation: The Vienna Convention Code as Applied by the World Trade Organization Judiciary," *Australian Year Book of International Law*, Vol. 20(1999), p. 334; Detlev F Vagts, "Treaty Interpretation and the New American Ways of Law Reading," *European Journal of International Law*, Vol. 4 (1993), p. 488.

[50] Arsalan M. Suleman, *supra* note 41, p. 222.

5.3.2 Object and Purpose

However, practice may also allow for liberal interpretation broadening the scope of the provision consistent with a treaty's *spirit*, though not language alone.[51] This flexibility stems from the general rule of interpretation codified in Article 31 of the Vienna Convention on the Law of Treaties, specifying interpretation considers object and purpose. Countries seeking to limit the spread of sensitive facilities argue Article IV remains subject to Articles I and II's overriding aim of curbing the spread of nuclear explosive devices.[52] A number of non-proliferation experts view sensitive activities as conflicting with the NPT's nonproliferation object and purpose, and therefore not within the "inalienable right."

Joseph Nye, then Deputy to the Under Secretary for Security Assistance, offered his legal defense of the U.S. policy deferring reprocessing: "… this decision does not mean that the U.S. has failed to support Article IV of the NPT. On the contrary, we recognize that, as a nuclear-weapon State, the U.S. has a special responsibility … Our policies are aimed to fulfill this responsibility, while directed against those activities proscribed in Articles I and II of the treaty. But in doing so, we must not imperil the *objectives* of Articles I and II."[53] (emphasis added).

Leonard S. Spector criticized the literal interpretation which would tolerate sensitive activities, arguing it "would make a mockery of their [non-nuclear States'] commitments to renounce nuclear weapons," and "…the NPT commitment not to 'manufacture' nuclear weapons incorporates a prohibition on all related development, component fabrication, and testing … firmly establishing the illegality of such activities under the NPT."[54] Lovins and Ross went even farther to suggest precluding not only sensitive nuclear activities but nuclear power altogether, since safeguards cannot fully prevent proliferation.[55] While acknowledging Article IV's ambiguity, Lovins and Ross insist that Article IV is "by its own terms subject to conformity with the primary obligation of the same treaty," arguing "nuclear power is something which under Article I the givers mustn't give and under Article II the recipients shouldn't ask for."[56]

In February 2004, U.S. President George W. Bush announced the "New Measures to Counter the Threat of WMD" speech.[57] Bush noted that the "treaty [NPT] has a

---

[51] Clovis C. Morrisson, Jr., *supra* note 49, p. 374.

[52] Ronald J. Bettauer, "The Nuclear Non-Proliferation Act of 1978," *Law and Policy in International Business*, Vol. 10 (1978), p. 1110.

[53] Joseph Nye, "United States Policy on Nuclear Technology: Combining Energy and Security," *State Department Bulletin*, Vol. 76 (1977), pp. 551–552.

[54] Leonard S. Spector, "Repentant Nuclear Proliferants," in William M. Evan and Ved P. Nanda eds., *Nuclear Proliferation and the Legality of Nuclear Weapons* (University Press of America, 1995), pp. 23–24.

[55] Amory B. Lovins, L. Hunter Lovins and Leonard Ross, "Nuclear Power and Nuclear Bombs," *Foreign Affairs*, Vol. 58 (1979–1980), p. 1146.

[56] *Ibid.*, p. 1169.

[57] Available at <http://www.whitehouse.gov/news/releases/2004/02/20040211-4.html >

loophole which has been exploited by nations such as North Korea and Iran. These regimes are allowed to produce nuclear material that can be used to build bombs under the cover of civilian nuclear programs." The referenced loophole stems from the interpretation of the "inalienable right" in Article IV. Bush proposed "a way to close the loophole" by denying enrichment/reprocessing rights to non-NSG state, asserting "enrichment and reprocessing are not necessary for (these) nations seeking to harness nuclear energy for peaceful purposes."[58] While this selective policy had long been implicitly applied regarding sensitive activities in Japan, Germany and other developed non-nuclear weapon states, Bush's speech marked the first explicit mention of such an "interpretation" of Article IV of the NPT. Bush did not intend to modify the clause, he simply put forth a reinterpretation to close the loophole.[59] Although criticism argues this contravenes the NPT's foundation whereby non-nuclear states relinquish weapons in exchange for peaceful nuclear technology use under safeguards,[60] the selective approach's framing as an interpretive means to fulfill the treaty's objectives could still align with its aims.[61]

5.3.3 Subsequent Practice and Review Conferences

Article VIII.3 of the NPT establishes the Review Conferences to examine treaty operation and ensure objectives are met.[62] While review processes are undefined, this novel concept was introduced during drafting to address potential objections from the non-nuclear-weapon states, potentially granting them bargaining power for satisfactory implementation of Article IV as well as effective operation of Article VI on nuclear arms control.[63] As far as the function of the Review Conferences in the NPT interpretation is concerned, it is widely accepted that the NPT Review Conference final declarations, while not binding, may aid legal interpretation as "subsequent agreements" and/or "subsequent practice" under Article 31(3) of the Vienna Convention on the Law of Treaties.[64] This approach to interpretation has also been

---

[58] *Ibid.*

[59] For the perspective advocating for a selective approach within academic discourse, see Lee Feinstein and Ann-Marie Slaughter, "A Duty to Prevent," *Foreign Affairs*, Vol. 83, (2004), pp. 136–146.

[60] Natasha Bajema and Mary Beth Nikitin, *supra* note 45, p. 166. Richard Falk notes that this kind of selective policy has "several detrimental effects on world order and opportunities for peace and security that are especially unfortunate within the current historical settings ... diminishes the legitimacy of world order; and it reflects a posture that contradicts the mandates of international law, international morality, and political consensus of the states...". See Richard Falk, *supra* note 27, p. 74.

[61] Thomas L. Neff and Henry D. Jacoby, *supra* note 16, p. 1139.

[62] Treaty on the Nonproliferation of Nuclear Weapons, *supra* note 11, Article VIII.3.

[63] Ben Sanders, "The Relevance of the NPT Process for Today's Proliferation and Disarmament Challenges," available at <http://cns.miis.edu/research/npt/pdf/workshop/wk_sand.pdf>.

[64] David S. Jonas, "The New U.S. Approach to the Fissile Material Cutoff Treaty: Will Deletion of a Verification Regime Provide a Way out of the Wilderness," *Florida Journal of International Law*,

suggested for the Biological Weapons Convention to clarify Article I prohibition. In this case, if the Final Document of a BWC Review Conference adopts certain interpretations by consensus, such interpretations will be valid and binding upon all BWC parties.[65] Let us briefly examine the NPT Review Conferences declarations on Articles II and IV to determine if any consensus was reached clarifying the scope of the prohibited "manufacture" or the inalienable right.

Since sensitive nuclear activities had not emerged as a salient issue, Article IV was not deliberated in the first Review Conference held in 1975. The 1980 NPT Review Conference failed to make a Final Declaration on the topic. The first official NPT States Party response to unilateral and multilateral control on sensitive nuclear activities thus came at the 1985 NPT Review Conference. While majority attitudes toward nuclear control were negative, the Final Declaration on Article IV only confirmed that the "inalienable right" should be respected: "…The Conference confirms that each country's choices and decisions in the field of peaceful uses of nuclear energy should be respected without jeopardizing their *respective fuel-cycle policies*…."[66] (not able to specify any sensitive part, emphasis added).

The 1990 Review Conferences again failed to produce any Final Declarations due to lack of consensus. Wording similarly "confirming" the Article IV "inalienable right" as was included in the 1985 version appeared in the 1995 NPT Review and Extension Conference,[67] the 2000 Final Document,[68] and the Report of the Preparatory Committee on its Second Session for the 2005 Review Conference.[69]

It is puzzling that while seeking to clarify Article IV's ambiguous text through review, the Review Conferences only restated this language without further resolution. Developing countries evidently made efforts in pre-conference meetings advocating against "unjust restrictions and constraints imposed on developing non-nuclear-weapon States regarding the *full access* to nuclear technology for peaceful purposes."[70] (emphasis added). However, discussions on Article IV of the NPT at

---

Vol. 18 (2006), p. 634; See also Patricia Hewitson, "Nonproliferation and Reduction of Nuclear Weapons: Risks of Weakening the Multilateral Nuclear Nonproliferation Norm," *Berkeley Journal of International Law*, Vol. 21 (2003), p. 445, p. 485.

[65] Burrus M. Carnahan and Katherine L. Starr, *supra* note 5, p. 633.

[66] U.N. Doc. NPT/CONF.III/64/I (September 21, 1985).

[67] Decision 2, para. 14–17, U.N. Doc. NPT/CONF.1995/32 (Part I) (May 11, 1995), pp. 11–12.

[68] Final Document Vol. I, U.N. Doc. NPT/CONF.2000/28 (Part I and Part II) (May 20, 2000), pp. 8–9.

[69] U.N. Doc. NPT/CONF.2005/PC.II/50 (May 13, 2003), para. 41.

[70] "Document on Substantive Issues submitted by Indonesia on behalf of the group of Non-Aligned and Other States," (1994), cited in Charles Van Doren, *supra* note 17, p. 19. See also the position of Iran on the issue, "NPT 'PrepCom' makes progress despite delays in final decision," Arms Control Today, Oct. 1994, p. 21. For the disputes between Iran and the U.S. in the NPT Preparatory Committee meeting for the 1995 NPT Review and Extension Conference in Geneva in September 1994, see Joseph F. Pilat and Charles W. Nakhleh, "A Treaty Reborn? The NPT After Extension," in Raju G.C. Thomas ed., *The Nuclear Non-proliferation Regime: Prospects for the 21st Century* (Macmillan Press, 1998), pp. 47–48. In the 2000 Review Conference, Non-Aligned Movement Countries announced: "The State Parties reaffirmed that beyond safeguards required under the Treaty; unilaterally enforced restrictive measures which prevent peaceful nuclear development

the 1995 Review Conference proved neither unexpected nor conclusive.[71] The final documents on reviewing Article IV mirrored only the 1985 language.

Indeed, of ten past Review Conferences, five failed to produce final declarations, including the pivotal 1995 NPT Review and Extension Conference.[72] The difficulties in reaching consensus through Review Conferences illustrate that while compromises allowing review of certain Articles occured, these resolutions provide little clarification given their nature as negotiated compromises.[73]

5.4 Conclusion

The unsettled interpretative issue appears from time to time in non-proliferation politics through States' conflicting autointerpretations. An example includes differences between the U.S. and its allies in the 1970s regarding sovereignty and restrictive, textual reading versus object and purpose readings, as seen today in the Iranian nuclear problem and the North Korean nuclear crisis. While both perspectives reference methods codified in the general rule of interpretation, the general rule appears to provide grounds for divergence rather than preclude disputes.

States are obliged to observe the general rule of interpretation as parties to the Vienna Convention on the Law of Treaties or under customary law. Examining observance may assess legal implications. However, the general rule of interpretation codified in Article 31 of the Vienna Convention on the Law of Treaties seems to offer little clarification for the ambiguous "inalienable right" in Article IV of the NPT. While a textual approach could support restrictive interpretations, a teleological approach leads to elsewhere, and subsequent practice brought nothing but ambiguity and confusion. Completely different conclusions on the interpretation of the "inalienable right" appear drawable by referencing Article 31 alone. Adherence to the VCLT rules seems illusory, resulting in "non-binding" characterizations of purportedly authoritative autointerpretations.[74]

---

should be removed." See "Working Paper for the NPT 2000 Review Conference Prepared by the Members of the Movement of Non-aligned Countries Parties to the Treaty on the Nonproliferation of Nuclear Weapons," New York, 24, April 2000.

[71] Lewis A. Dunn, "High Noon for the NPT," *Arms Control Today*, Vol. 25 (1995), p. 8.

[72] The 1995 Review and Extension Conference produced linked package of three decisions and one resolution at the expense of a final declaration. See William C. Potter, "The NPT Review Conference: 188 States in Search of Consensus," *The International Spectator* Vol. 3(2005), p. 20.

[73] Some experts suggest that the NPT should have more meaningful review mechanisms than that currently in operation. See Arsalan M. Suleman, *supra* note 41, p. 229.

[74] Leo Gross, "States as Organs of International Law and the Problem of Autointerpretation," *Essays on International Law and Organization* (Springer, 1984), pp. 368–369.

The divergence between theoretical guidelines and practical application suggests the general rule of interpretation offers little predictive value regarding specific autointerpretations' legal implications. Reasonably, this prompts examining whether theoretical limitations exist concerning the general rule of interpretation, and if so, how their influence could be mitigated.

Chapter 6
The Riddle of Treaty Interpretation

6.1 Introduction

Today, international law is undergoing so-called "fragmentation." Examples of this phenomenon related to treaty law include such commentary as "the treaty rule is unclear or open-textured" and "concepts used in the treaty are open or evolving."[1] Prosper Weil regarded this phenomenon as part of "relative normativity," referring to some weak, vague or poorly drafted contents in binding instruments as "soft law."[2] Dinah Shelton concluded that such "soft law," in the normative hierarchy of the international legal system, "seems more appropriate for the more hortatory or promotional language of certain treaty provisions."[3] In the field of arms control, these two versions of soft law in binding documents have been characterized as "the use of indeterminate language in key provisions."[4] Case studies in arms control treaties indicate that key clauses in these treaties suffer from problems of indeterminate language,[5] though

[1] Conclusions of the work of the Study Group on the Fragmentation of International Law: Difficulties arising from the Diversification and Expansion of International Law, available at, <https://legal.un.org/ilc/texts/instruments/english/draft_articles/1_9_2006.pdf>.

[2] Prosper Weil, "Towards Relative Normativity in International Law?" *American Journal of International Law*, Vol. 77 (1983), p. 414.

[3] Dinah Shelton, "Normative Hierarchy in International Law," *American Journal of International Law*, Vol. 100 (2006), p. 319.

[4] Jack M. Beard, "The Shortcomings of Indeterminacy in Arms Control Regimes: The Case of the Biological Weapons Convention," *American Journal of International Law*, Vol. 101 (2007), p. 273.

[5] Jack Beard only considered the Biological Weapons Convention (the "BWC") as a case study on the problem of indeterminate language. See Jack Beard, *ibid*., pp. 281–282. On the same problem, see also Burrus M. Carnahan and Katherine L. Starr, "Law and Policy in the Amendment of Arms Control Agreements," *Loyola of Los Angeles International and Comparative Law Review*, Vol. 20 (1997–1998), pp. 632–633. Eric Stein examined the ambiguous provisions and interpretative problems in various arms control treaties, for example, the "peaceful purpose" and non-militarization in Article 1 of the Antarctic Treaty, the first paragraph of Article IV of the Outer Space Treaty, the object of prohibition in Article 1 of the Sea Bed Treaty, "the presence of radioactive debris" in

X. Zhang, *Law and Politics in Peaceful Use of Nuclear Energy*,
https://doi.org/10.1007/978-981-97-3813-7_6

few studies have considered the difference between text that prescribes obligation but is ambiguous and language of a hortatory or promotional nature.

Treaty interpretation, more precisely, the application of a general rule of treaty interpretation codified in the Vienna Convention on the Law of Treaties, looks to be a myth to many international lawyers. However, I argue that the myth is made by those on the basis of rule-oriented legal thinking, and this legal thinking can only acquire validity on the basis of some limited prepositions. In my view, treaty interpretation is not a myth that subject to no resolution by human being but a riddle that can be approached from broader perspectives on the rules and norms in international relations.

This chapter will first examine theoretical limitations and pitfalls of the general rule of interpretation codified in the 1969 Vienna Convention on the Law of Treaties. Observations will then consider how the general rule of interpretation was introduced by positivist international lawyers and why it became problematic—the problems of positivist methodology employed by the positivist international lawyers in codifying this general rule of interpretation. The discussion will also explore research on rules and norms in international relations, drawing from tenets of Constructivists, to further elucidate the nuanced "riddle" of treaty interpretation.

6.2 The General Rule of Interpretation: Limits and Theoretical Pitfalls

The failure or the myth of treaty interpretation can be explained by two contributing factors. First, the object of the interpretation is not suitable for interpretation (more specifically, for the application of the general rule of interpretation)—in a sense it is un-interpretable. Second, the law of interpretation, namely the general rule of interpretation, is not capable of handling the difficult task of interpretation. Though these two factors may be considered separately, they are indeed inter-related, exacerbating symptoms of "fragmentation" within treaty law.

6.2.1 The Object—Un-interpretable?

Many international lawyers believe that the methods or rules of interpretation are to be chosen in accordance with the subject matter of the treaty to be interpreted.[6] This implies that any defined rule of interpretation may have very limited application

Article 1(1) b of PTBT. See Eric Stein, "Legal Restraints in Modern Arms Control Agreements," *American Journal of International Law*, Vol. 66 (1972), pp. 258–267.

[6] Francis G. Jacobs, "Varieties of Approach to Treaty Interpretation: With Special Reference to the Draft Convention on the Law of Treaties before the Vienna Diplomatic Conference," *International and Comparative Law Quarterly*, Vol. 18 (1969), p. 320.

to a certain subject matter. Therefore, a defined rule of interpretation is doomed to be incompetent at handling a specific object of interpretation (provisions in certain categories of treaties) if it is applied in an alien context. By this thread of reasoning, an argument on the present interpretation issue would be that the "inalienable right" (object) in Article IV of the NPT is not suitable for the application of the general rule of interpretation codified in Article 31 of the Vienna Convention on the Law of Treaties (law). This argument requires an examination of both the nature of the object as well as the law of interpretation.

Is the "inalienable right" un-interpretable? If we regard interpretation in international law as a pure judicial process, the answer may be yes, because the object of interpretation is often "political" in nature,[7] and therefore cannot be governed by the law of interpretation. The problem of this argument is that it relies mostly on the domestic law model and ignores the reality of the international legal system, where both political organs and judicial organs are less developed and thus issues straddle both spheres with an indiscernible dividing line, especially in the domain of arms control (for example, the Legality of the Threat or Use of Nuclear Weapons Case).

As a matter of fact, the general rule of interpretation, though itself relied heavily on the past judicial decisions when it was being codified into the draft Article 27 of the Vienna Convention on the Law of Treaties by the International Law Commission (ILC), it was nevertheless not intended merely for judicial purposes when it was finally deliberated and adopted as Article 31 of the Vienna Convention on the Law of Treaties at the Vienna Conference. The rationale behind the international society incorporating an interpretation rule into the law is that, in an international legal system, interpretation is, in most cases, a matter of autointerpretation,[8] so an explicit rule of interpretation is useful in preventing disputes from arising in autointerpretation,[9] but not necessarily for settling a dispute.[10] Indeed, such dispute resolution is the main purpose of judicial process in domestic legal systems. In this sense, Article 31 of the Vienna Convention on the Law of Treaties is to a great extent a norm of

---

[7] Especially in the domain of arms control which is regarded as "fundamentally a political process." See Ian Johnstone, "Treaty Interpretation: The Authority of Interpretive Communities," *Michigan Journal of International Law*, Vol. 12 (1990–1991), p. 394.

[8] *Ibid.*, pp. 371–372. In general, see also Leo Gross, "States as Organs of International Law and the Problem of Autointerpretation," *Essays on international law and organization* (Springer, 1984), pp. 368–369.

[9] Francis G. Jacobs, *supra* note 6, p. 342; Shabtai Rosenne, "Interpretation of Treaties in the Restatement and the International Law Commission's Draft Articles: A Comparison," *Columbia Journal of Transnational Law*, Vol. 5 (1966), p. 226; As Georg Schwarzenberger correctly pointed out, despite the VCLT's adoption, disputes over treaty interpretation are unlikely to be resolved by international courts given their limited compulsory jurisdiction. Rather, conflicting views are more probable during the state of auto-interpretation by parties. Therefore, the paramount aim should be to promote agreement and avoid divergent interpretations between states. See Georg Schwarzenberger, "Myths and Realities of Treaty Interpretation: Articles 27–29 of the Vienna Draft Convention on the Law of Treaties," *Virginia Journal of International Law*, Vol. 9 (1968–1969), p. 18.

[10] D. W. Greig, *International Law* (2nd ed, Butterworths, 1976), p. 477. (noting that judicial settlement remains the exception in international disputes, as political compromise frequently determines the agreed "meaning" of contested treaty terms).

conduct, and should be applied even when the object of interpretation is "political" in nature.

The true challenge in interpreting the "inalienable right" potentially stems from linguistic indeterminacy within the language used. Unfortunately, doctrinal debate to date may have inadvertently obfuscated understanding on this issue.

The prevailing argument in the doctrinal debate over language indeterminacy, while asserted as a rebuttable presumption, maintains that the interpreter is "entirely justified in assuming that the treaty means what it says and says what it means."[11] Gross argues that it is unrealistic to assume that states would use language fully expressing their intentions or genuine shared expectations.[12] He reasons:

> ...words may not be an ideally precise method of communication.... But we should not overlook altogether the fact that the modern treaty making process involves many opportunities for control. The prospect of a treaty with a certain state is carefully considered in many government departments before being taken up with it; it may go through several drafts before it is incorporated in a final text; this text is again carefully scrutinized in several government departments, in hearing before the Senate (in this country [the U.S.]) or Parliament, by the Senate itself and finally it is still open to the states to withhold ratification or attach reservations.[13]

Critical Legal Study ("CLS") scholars highlight linguistic indeterminacy as a key critique of doctrinal approaches. Onuf argued for a constitutive relationship between individuals, society and rules mediated through language.[14] His post-positivist social theory rejects singular truths as they are "inextricable from the arguments offered for."[15] Koskenniemi launched the Deconstructionist perspective on the phenomenon of language indeterminacy. His central argument is that international law is irredeemably indeterminate because it is predicated on the conceptual opposition of apology and utopia.[16]

While CLS scholars raise valid questions regarding linguistic uncertainty, some argue their framing of the issue as inherently exaggerated. Iain Scobbie once aptly

---

[11] Leo Gross, "Treaty Interpretation: The Proper Role of an International Tribunal," *American Society of International Law Proceedings*, Vol. 63 (1969), p. 121.

[12] *Ibid.*, p. 120.

[13] *Ibid.*, p. 121.

[14] Nicholas Onuf, "The Constitution of International Politics," *European Journal of International Law*, Vol. 5, No. 1 (1994), p. 4.

[15] Nicholas Onuf, *World of Our Making: Rules and Rule in Social Theory and International Relations* (University of South Carolina Press, 1989), p. 35.

[16] M. Koskenniemi, *From Apology to Utopia; the Structure of International Legal Argument* (Coronet Books, 1989), p. 42. For deconstructionists, concepts are constituted through the opposition of contrasting ideas—for instance, in relation to international law, Koskenniemi argues that internal contradictions arise through the opposition of natural law and positivism, world communality and State sovereignty. In order to define or describe concepts, arguments attempt to establish the priority of one or other term of the contrasting pair in issue, but deconstruction maintains that such priority cannot be definitely established because the terms of the pair are not fundamentally in opposition to each other but are dependent upon one another. See Iain Scobbie, "Towards the Elimination of International Law: Some Radical Skepticism about Skeptical Radicalism" *British Yearbook of International Law*, Vol. 61 (1990), p. 340.

commented on Koskenniemi's *From Apology to Utopia*: if language is indeterminate, what is the point to write the book?[17]

Neither simplifying language's nature nor exaggerating its ambiguity fully captures treaty making realities. If language is truly indeterminate, why do sovereign States negotiate so hard on treaty text? While positivist international lawyers emphasize textual clarity, other important factors likely influence state negotiations making treaty text ambiguous and contradictory. Chayes observed:

> Treaty drafters do not foresee many of the possible applications—let alone their contextual setting. Issues that are foreseen often cannot be resolved at the time of treaty negotiation and are swept under the rug with a formula that can mean what each party wants it to mean. Economic, technological, scientific, and even political circumstances change. All these inescapable incidents of the effort to formulate rules to govern future conduct frequently produce a zone of ambiguity within which it is difficult to say with precision what is permitted and what is forbidden.[18]

In essence, language serves as both a means of communication and medium for making treaty rules. However, it can also be intentionally used not only to mean what has been agreed, but also to imply unsettled discrepancies between negotiating States through deliberately crafted ambiguity within agreed text.[19] In modern treaty making practice, lawyers (legal advisers) directly participate in or lead negotiations, undermining claims that imperfect treaty provisions stem solely from deficiencies in legal expertise.[20] Rather, textual ambiguity is intentionally made by the negotiating States; it is a product of what is called "intentional ambiguity" elsewhere.[21]

This intentional ambiguity may complicate interpretation in the international legal system grounded in state sovereignty and equality. As international law derives authority from consent of the sovereign states,[22] textual intention holds significance. Yet if language indeterminacy allows States to keep discrepancies while maintaining "agreement" on text, determining a norm's true meaning through interpretive rules could contravene state will. It may be argued that the general rule of interpretation (Article 31 of the Vienna Convention on the Law of Treaties) also assumes discernible legislative intention underlining an "interpretable" treaty provision. However, this proposition may not always reflect realities of modern treaty-making.

It must be noted that while language indeterminacy is a necessary condition, it alone does not determine an object's interpretability. As such, debates fixating solely on language indeterminacy risks being counterproductive and failing to address why

---

[17] Iain Scobbie, *ibid.*, p. 346.

[18] Abram Chayes and Antonia Handler Chayes, "On Compliance," *International Organization*, Vol. 47 (1993), pp. 188–189.

[19] Francis G. Jacobs, *supra* note 6, p. 339; Gidon Gottlieb, "The Interpretation of Treaties by Tribunals," *American Society of International Law Proceedings*, Vol. 63 (1969), p. 130.

[20] Detlev F Vagts, "Treaty Interpretation and the New American Ways of Law Reading," *European Journal of International Law*, Vol. 4 (1993), p. 476.

[21] See discussion in Chap. 3 of this study.

[22] Detlev F. Vagts, *supra* note 20, p. 504.

certain objects of interpretation are "un-interpretable". The validity of an interpretive proposition, in these cases, does not inherently implicate the interpretive process itself but rather represents a factual inquiry into negotiators' rationale for deliberately crafting imprecise language.

Therefore, whether an intentional ambiguity exists represents a factual inquiry best addressed by examining evidence from the *travaux préparatoires*. The relevant consideration is not interpreting collective drafter intent or reconciling conflicting intentions implied by text, as travaux préparatoires only partially inform interpretation based on intention (the so called school of intention).[23] Rather, the objective is ascertaining the common intention of the drafters in keeping ambiguity in the text of the treaty despite potential clarity cost. Since doing so extends beyond the textual analysis associated with interpretation, this type of intent ascertainment should be considered separately from matters of legal interpretation *per se*.

As for "intentional ambiguity" regarding the "inalienable right," a thorough examination of the *travaux préparatoires* on Article IV of the NPT was undertaken in Chap. 3. The research produced the following key findings:

> In the case of the NPT negotiation, even countries that made efforts to clarify the draft, eventually found them satisfied, or compromised with the ambiguity. Revisiting the NPT negotiation also showed a strong intention of the dominant players (such as the U.S.), in advocating for such an ambiguity. The intentionally drafted ambiguity seemed to be tolerated by dissenting countries.[24]

6.2.2 *The Law—Quis Custodiet Ipsos Custodes?*

The second factor accountable for the failure of interpretation can be attributed to the law, namely the general rule of interpretation. D. P. O'Connell had before foreseen this problem:

> Article[s] 31–33 ... has the effect of transforming logical positions into rules of law. However, the priority inherent in the application of these rules are not clearly indicated, and the rules themselves are in part so general that it is necessary to review traditional methods whenever interpreting a treaty. The danger in these rules is that States will argue that they are comprehensive of the canons of interpretation, whereas they are selective and themselves ambiguous. More controversy is likely to be aroused by them than allayed.[25]

McDougal also noted that Articles 31–33 of the Vienna Convention on the Law of Treaties, in being entirely eclectic and embracing all interpretative approaches,[26] were "so vague and imprecise and so impossible of effective application" that they merely "create myth for cloaking arbitrary decision."[27]

---

[23] *Ibid.*, p. 504.

[24] See the concluding remark in Chap. 3.

[25] D. P. O'Connell, *International Law* (2nd ed. Stevens, 1970), p. 253.

[26] Myres S. McDougal, "The International Law Commission's Draft Articles upon Interpretation: Textuality Redivivus," *American Journal of International Law*, Vol. 61 (1967), p. 992.

[27] *Ibid.*, p. 998.

Do laws of interpretation make interpretation in international law a myth? If so, what is the theoretical pitfall of such myth?

The law, or more precisely, the "general rule of treaty interpretation" in Article 31, does not exclude consideration of extra-textual elements such as "object and purpose" and "subsequent practice." As the International Law Commission noted, Article 31's structure does not establish a legal hierarchy, and use of the singular "general rule" rather than plural "rules" suggests interpretation involves a uniform, integrated process.[28] While there may be a "consideration of logic," the Commission affirmed the "starting point of interpretation is the meaning of the text."[29]

The Commission only provided guidance on the logical "starting point" for the interpretation but did not explain where the interpretation should end—the text, object and purpose, and subsequent practices are all suitable areas for interpretation. In doctrinal discussions, one view holds the text itself as the rigid "endpoint," as in Vattel's principle of *le sens clair*—unambiguous language requires no further interpretation.[30] However, as McDougal argued, "the determination of what text does or does not require interpretation is in itself an interpretation."[31]

The process of treaty interpretation with treaty text as the starting point then looks like a "magic box" in practice. Upon entering the text into one side, the outcome upon exit remains unknown due to interpretation's integrated, uniform approach considering multiple factors. In Leo Gross's words, "... the text is the 'starting point' of interpretation. Whether it will become its 'ending point' depends upon other elements of interpretation."[32]

Ultimately, how can one know the exact content of the "general rule of interpretation" prescribed in Article 31 of the Vienna Convention on the Law of Treaties when using it to interpret a treaty provision? A purely interpretive perspective cannot provide an answer, as it would be circular reasoning to interpret a rule of interpretation that itself establishes norms governing treaty interpretation.[33] This paradox has been referred to as *Quis custodiet ipsos custodes*.[34] Relying exclusively on

---

[28] *Yearbook of the International Law Commission 1966* Vol. II, pp. 219–220.

[29] *Ibid.*, p.220.

[30] Emmerich de Vattel, *The Law of Nations or the Principles of Natural Law*, p. 199, cited in Edward Slavko Yambrusic, *Treaty Interpretation: Theory and Reality* (University Press of America, 1987), p. 9.

[31] Myers S. McDougal, "Statement of Professor Myers S. McDougal, United States Delegation, to Committee of the Whole, April 19, 1968," *American Journal of International Law*, Vol. 62 (1968), p. 1023. Similarly, Lauterpacht wrote in 1935, "an expression is clear is—or ought to be—the result of the process of interpretation, not the starting point." See H. Lauterpacht, "Some Observations on Preparatory Work in the Interpretation of Treaties," *Harvard Law Review*, Vol. 48 (1935), p. 573.

[32] Leo Gross, *supra* note 11, p. 119.

[33] Gidon Gottlieb, *supra* note 19, p. 124 (noting that the ILC draft Articles 27 and 28 do not give us much help in interpreting their own provisions); G. G Lawrie, "Application and Interpretation of the Vienna Convention on the Law of Treaties", *Hong Kong Law Journal*, Vol. 2 (1972), p. 273 (noting that this is particular evident in the VCLT provisions governing treaty interpretation—Articles 31, 32 and 33—which themselves give rise to difficult questions of interpretation).

[34] G. G. Lawrie, *ibid.*, p. 275; Gerald Fitzmaurice, "Vae Victis or Woe to the Negotiators—Your Treaty or Our Interpretation of It", *American Journal of International Law*, Vol. 65 (1971), p. 361.

a treaty-based rule risks reducing interpretation to a "myth" susceptible to circularity critiques,[35] with no independent means to clarify the rule's own meaning and application.

Indeed, there has long been considerable skepticism from both commentators and practitioners regarding the very existence[36] and utility of treaty interpretive norms.[37] An insightful observation made by Lauterpacht in 1935 remians convincing:

> For reasons peculiar to the international judicial function, it is particularly true to say that in the matter of interpretation of treaties the absence of definite and elaborate rules means not arbitrariness and anarchy but the fulfillment of the purpose of the law as agreed by the parties.[38]

At the core, interpretation especially in a judicial sense, is "an intellectual process that does not lend itself to a strict legal formulization."[39] It is therefore unsurprising that domestic law refrains from codifying rigid interpretive norms, where the interpretation process is mainly a judicial activity and thus up to the judges to choose the methods or principles for their interpretation. While international law understandably includes an explicit rule to guide states own *ex post* "autointerpretations," the complexity of interpretation as an intellectual process makes comprehensive control through codification challenging. Even the International Law Commission acknowleged treaty interpretation "to some extent [as] an art, not an exact science."[40]

6.3 Insufficiency of Rule-Oriented Legal Thinking and the Problems of the Rule of Interpretation

The previous discussion highlighted how intentional ambiguity in treaty language and the creation of dynamic obligations that evolve with changing circumstances pose challenges for a strictly rule-based interpretive approach. If states have given their consent during treaty making to create dynamic obligations, rigidly defining meaning runs counter to their intent. Additionally, it appears to be a paradox inherent in the codified textual-contextual rule of treaty interpretation. Taken together, these

---

[35] See in general, Georg Schwarzenberger, *supra* note 9; Shigeki Sakamoto, "Jyoyaku Kaishyaku No shinwa To Genjitsu [Myth and Reality of Treaty Interpretation: What does the end of conflicting doctrine of interpretation mean?]" *Sekaiho Nenpo [Year Book of World Law]*, Vol. 22 (2003) pp. 30–61.

[36] Sir Hersh Lauterpacht, "Restrictive Interpretation and the Principle of Effectiveness in the Interpretation of Treaties," *British Yearbook of International Law*, Vol. 26 (1949), p. 48, p. 53. See also Myers S. McDougal, *supra* note 31, p. 1022. The ILC also took note of this position espoused in academic debate, see ILC Yearbook, *supra* note 28, p. 218.

[37] Gerald P. McGinley, "Practice as a Guide to Treaty Interpretation," *Fletcher Forum*, Vol. 9 (1985), pp. 211–212.

[38] H. Lauterpacht, *supra* note 31, p. 591.

[39] Edward Slavko Yambrusic, *supra* note 30, p. 249.

[40] ILC Yearbook, *supra* note 28, p. 218.

issues suggest reexamining presumptions underlying the articulation of general interpretive norms from a positivist, rule-focused perspective.

6.3.1 Rule-Oriented Legal Thinking and the Codified General Rule of Interpretation

Rule-oriented legal thinking commonly presumes an objective world can be described and interstate relations can be defined and regulated by a set of static rules. Considerable questions remain regarding these presumptions: Is reality truly objective enough to be fully captured by static norms? How scientifically valid is the positivist method of identifying rules? Can we use a "scientific method"—collecting and observing samples establishing effectiveness—in finding a rule of treaty interpretation given the intellectual, contextual nature of the task?

The task of a rule-oriented approach is to discover the law through objective evidence like treaty text. By focusing on examining the text and the context of the treaty provision, it is apparently a text-context approach. Rule-oriented legal thinking prioritizes a legal–illegal judgment that relies on a presumption that the content of the law was fixed at the point of treaty conclusion and can be clarified by the rule of interpretation. In addition, rule-oriented legal thinking believes that the static rules regulate the states' behavior—emphasizing the regulative nature of rules and norms in international relations.

Let's first turn to the methodology of rule-oriented legal thinking and the codification of a general rule of treaty interpretation. Nearly a century ago, Oppenheim advocated applying a "method of the science of international law" to fulfill the aim of discerning existing rules of law.[41] Regarding treaty rules, Oppenheim put forth the following optimistic perspective:

> In so far as conventional rules are concerned, it is to a certain extent easy to find them. They are written rules. Their scope, their meaning, and their extent in many cases can be grasped at a first glance. If we only possess accurate copies of the authentic documents, in which these rules are embodied, and if we are able to master the language in which these documents are drawn up, we often get at their meaning without great difficulty. But frequently they nevertheless present doubt and uncertainty enough, and then they require interpretation, … However this may be, written rules never offer such great difficulties to the science of international law as rules based on custom.[42]

Building upon Oppenheim's science of international law, McNair's seminal work several decades later examined the positivists' understanding of the Law of Treaties.[43] In the work, McNair investigated a wide range of international judicial judgments, domestic court decisions, and states' practices regarding the law of treaties. From

---

[41] Lassa Oppenheim, "The Science of International Law: Its Task and Method," *American Journal of International Law*, Vol. 2 (1908), p. 315.

[42] *Ibid.*, 334.

[43] Lord McNair, *The Law of Treaties* (Oxford at the Clarendon Press, 1961).

this comprehensive analysis, the rule of treaty interpretation was induced favoring a textual-contextual approach of treaty interpretation.

In the years following publication of McNair's The Law of Treaties, four English international lawyers serving on the International Law Commission—J. L. Brierly, H. Lauterpacht, G. Fitzmaurice, and H. Waldock— presided over drafting the rule of treaty interpretation at the Vienna Convention on the Law of Treaties. McNair's text-context approach representing the dominant English positivist perspective, proved influential as those provisions took form.

The rule of treaty interpretation is viewed as a customary rule codified in the Vienna Convention.[44] It can be identified by the positivist method of identifying a customary rule. This rule of treaty interpretation was identified and codified in the 1969 Vienna Convention through the effort of English international lawyers.

6.3.2 *Methodological Problems*

The positivist method of identifying a customary rule, with its most salient manner of an inductive approach,[45] favors deriving legal rules by examining their practical effect through states' actions and perspectives. However, questions remain regarding this approach in ascertaining and codifying the rule of treaty interpretation.

The first question is, when using this inductive method, what constitutes appropriate "samples" given the diversity of state practice in this area. When the ILC used the inductive method to identify rules of treaty interpretation, "samples" are mainly those from domestic and international judicial cases. This represents a "juridical filter" that both narrows the data and risks distorting the results by focusing solely on limited case outcomes rather than the full range of real-world state practice in treaty interpretation—states themselves are the ultimate arbiters in deciding whether any individual international law exists and how they will apply it.[46]

Firstly, the number of cases concerning treaty interpretation from which the rule of treaty interpretation may be induced has been greatly reduced in the international judicial process because international judicial organs have jurisdiction only for cases that parties agreed to submit to them. When a case is initiated against a major state,

[44] Articles 31 and 32 are binding treaty law for parties to the Vienna Convention as well as codified rules of customary international law. See *Territorial Dispute (Libya v. Chad), Judgment,* I.C.J. Reports 1994, p. 19, para. 41. For an overall discussion on the codification of pre-existing customary law in Articles 31–33, see Evan Criddle, "The Vienna Convention on the Law of Treaties in U.S. Treaty Interpretation," *Virginia Journal of International Law*, Vol. 44 (2003–2004), pp. 445–448.

[45] Georg Schwarzenberger, "The Inductive Approach to International Law," *Harvard Law Review*, Vol. 60 (1946–1947), p. 562; Georg Schwarzenberger, *A Manual of International Law* (5th ed., London Institute of World Affairs by Stevens, 1967), p. 21.

[46] H. Lauterpacht, *The Function of Law in the International Community* (The Clarendon Press, 1933), p. 3. See also *Jaworzina, Advisory Opinion, December 6, 1923,* Series B, No. 8, p. 37 (The PCIJ referred to the "established principle that the right of giving an authorities interpretation of a legal rule belongs solely to the person or body who has the power to modify or suppress it.").

that state may be reluctant to subject itself to the jurisdiction of an international judicial organ. For example, in the 1986 International Court of Justice (ICJ) case *Military and Paramilitary Activities in and Against Nicaragua (Nicaragua v. United States)*, on receiving a jurisdictional judgment rejecting its objections, the United States as respondent decided to withdraw its declaration that it had given the ICJ its general consent to jurisdiction under the optional clause of the ICJ Statute.[47] Although in that instant case, the ICJ declined to recognize the immediate effect of the U.S. withdrawal of its declaration accepting jurisdiction under the same clause,[48] the U.S. withdrawal nevertheless came into effect later at some point. Since then, among the five permanent members of the UN Security Council, the United Kingdom still withholds its declaration made under the optional clause of the ICJ Statute.[49] Therefore, practices of major states in treaty interpretation are less likely to be used as samples in determining the customary rule on interpretation by using the juridical–inductive method.

Secondly, when a dispute concerning the interpretation of a particular treaty provision involves a state's vital national interests, that state would probably also oppose being subject to any third party dispute settlement mechanism. For example, when settling a dispute concerning the interpretation or application of the United Nations Convention on the Law of the Sea, Party States are entitled to exclude disputes concerning military activities from the obligatory judicial–arbitral process.[50] Indeed, contentious cases concerning security issues are rare. Since not many treaty interpretation samples are available in the field of national security, whether the inductive method employing a "juridical filter" can achieve its aim in identifying the customary rule of treaty interpretation remains dubious.

Thirdly, facing an interpretive issue arising from a treaty on security matters, the ICJ sometimes was reluctant to provide a solution. In the *Legality of the Threat or Use of Nuclear Weapons (Advisory Opinion)*, the International Court of Justice stated:

> … the threat or use of nuclear weapons would generally be contrary to the rules of international law applicable in armed conflict, and in particular the principles and rules of humanitarian law. However, in view of the current state of international law, and of the elements of fact at its disposal, *the Court cannot conclude definitively whether the threat or use of*

[47] *Military and Paramilitary Activities in and against Nicaragua (Nicaragua v. United States of America), Merits, Judgement,* I.C.J. Reports 1986, p. 17, para.10.

[48] *Military and Paramilitary Activities in and against Nicaragua (Nicaragua v. United States of America), Jurisdiction and Admissibility, Judgement,* I.C.J. Reports 1984, pp. 399–405, paras.16–28.

[49] Statute of the Court, I.C.J. Acts & Docs. (I.C.J. Statute), art. 36 (2)–(5), available at <http://www.icj-cij.org/en/statute>. France withdrew its declaration accepting the compulsory jurisdiction of the ICJ after being sued by Australia and New Zealand in the *Nuclear Test* cases. The other two permanent members of the Security Council, Russia (the former USSR) and the People's Republic of China, have not made declarations accepting the ICJ's jurisdiction pursuant to Article 36(2)–(5) of the ICJ Statute.

[50] United Nations Convention on the Law of the Sea, adopted December 10, 1982, entered into force November 16, 1994, 1833 UNTS. 397, art. 298(1)(b).

> *nuclear weapons would be lawful or unlawful in an extreme circumstance* of self-defense, in which the very survival of a State would be at stake.[51] (emphasis added).

Overall, the inadequacy of the samples poses a serious problem for determining the contents of the customary rule of interpretation using the inductive method. In particular, as long as the disputes over the interpretation or application of treaties on security matters are seldom accommodated by international judicial processes, universal application of the customary rule of treaty interpretation becomes problematic. As a result, the interpretation of treaties addressing security issues appears to be a difficult challenge to overcome.

The second problem with the inductive methodology is that, in codifying the general rule of treaty interpretation, the International Law Commission failed to provide precise guidance for treaty interpretation. The "general rule of treaty interpretation" favours a textual–contextual approach and uses the text as the starting point of the interpretation process but also acknowledges some extratextual factors (or interpretive approaches), viewing them as having logical connections in the interpretation process. As discussed in the preceding section, problems exist relating to the treaty interpretation process when applying the general rule of treaty interpretation: interpretation more or less appears as a "magic box" with the text of a treaty as the starting point; what comes out at the end of this process largely depends on the prevailing approach within this magic box.[52] The general rule of interpretation, when codified by the Vienna Convention on the Law of Treaties using the inductive method, can be said to reflect a compromise blending different approaches to treaty interpretation employed by various judicial forums, both international and domestic.

Domestic judicial cases of treaty interpretation demonstrate a variety of approaches. Yambrusic investigated domestic jurisprudence and found that, in common-law/socialist countries, courts implicitly recognized that extrinsic evidence carries a different weight in the interpretation process. However, in countries with a continental law system, the courts' interpretive approach is more favorable to the notion of rational objectivity: extrinsic evidence merely confirms the meaning primarily deduced from the textual context.[53] Regarding treaty interpretation in regional–domestic courts, a study also finds that different courts tend to interpret a treaty provision of the same subject matter in strikingly different manners. For example, when interpreting human rights conventions, Japanese courts usually employed a textual–contextual approach, whereas the European Court of Human Rights overwhelmingly favored an evolutionary interpretation.[54]

---

[51] *Legality of the Threat or Use of Nulcear Weapons, Advisory Opinion,* I.C.J. Reports 1996, p. 266, para. 105. Judge Oda in his dissenting opinion noted that the UN General Assembly submitted the question with highly political motives, arguing that the court should have declined from the outset to give any opinion at all in the case, p. 373.

[52] See accompanying text to *supra* note 32.

[53] Edward Slavko Yambrusic, *supra* note 30, p. 35.

[54] Shigeki Sakamoto, *supra* note 35, pp. 46–49.

In the implementation of the rule of interpretation in international judicial cases after the adoption of the 1969 Vienna Convention on the Law of Treaties, international courts and tribunals—when claiming that their interpretation was based on the general rule of treaty interpretation of Article 31 of the 1969 Vienna Convention—indeed arrived at different ending points. A survey of such an interpretation practice shows that the ICJ generally employs a textual–contextual approach. However, the European Court of Human Rights more often emphasizes "object and purpose" for treaty interpretation and sometimes employs an evolutionary approach in interpreting human rights conventions.[55]

The practice of international and domestic judicial forums in treaty interpretation demonstrates that the logical connections embedded in the general rule of treaty interpretation, referring to different approaches to treaty interpretation, are less relevant to the text of a treaty and more pertinent to regional and cultural contexts. Regional and cultural factors, rather than the "logic" of the rule of interpretation, appear to make a difference in determining the outcome of the treaty interpretation process. This finding perhaps reflects the very nature of treaty interpretation, as international lawyers widely acknowledge that interpretation is "an intellectual process that does not lend itself to a strict legal formulization,"[56] implicitly acknowledging the limitations of the inductive method used to derive the "general rule of treaty interpretation."

Having said so, the inductive method is strongly believed by some to be a scientific method in the sense that it is objective and immune to political bias.[57] In the view of the present author, this is the third problem with a strict positivist methodology. Indeed, the International Law Commission in its commentary on the draft articles pointed out that treaty interpretation was "to some extent an art, not an exact science."[58] This statement raises the question of how scientific the general rule of interpretation is, let alone how a scientific method can be employed in determining such a general rule of interpretation.

Taking treaty interpretation as an art, international courts and tribunals may find a better position in carrying out their functions when settling interstate disputes. The general rule of treaty interpretation—that it enables an objective judgment void of political bias—cannot be taken for granted. When a contentious case is submitted to a court or tribunal, the court or tribunal must adjudicate specific legal issues in which the parties have conflicting legal interests. The function of a court or tribunal is not to elucidate abstract principles but to offer the parties in dispute a legal solution. In a judgment leading to the settlement of a dispute, a court or tribunal must state reasons, including those on treaty interpretation, and the judgment only has binding force on the parties in that specific case.[59] Under such circumstances, a court or tribunal in

[55] *Ibid.*, pp. 38–46.

[56] Edward Slavko Yambrusic, *supra* note 30, p. 249.

[57] Prosper Weil, *supra* note 2, p. 420.

[58] ILC Yearbook, *supra* note 28, p. 218.

[59] Statute of the Court, I.C.J. Acts & Docs. (I.C.J. Statute), art. 59, available at <http://www.icj-cij.org/en/statute>.

a contentious case inclines to view the treaty provisions as static and regulative. By resorting to the text of the treaty to which the interpretation or application is in dispute, a court or tribunal is able to render a judgment and decide who is right and who is wrong and, thus regulating the behavior of the parties in dispute.

In doing so, a court or tribunal may find it unnecessary to examine the preliminary question of whether the dispute submitted to it arises from a dynamic commitment. Differences in the decision-making process (treaty making) that were maintained through agreement on dynamic treaty obligations are forced to be settled by applying the general rule of treaty interpretation, which ignores all unfinished political differences reflected in the agreement on dynamic treaty obligations. Overall, applying the general rule of interpretation codified in the Vienna Convention on the Law of Treaties is not aimed at achieving a scientific conclusion for judicial settlement.

In general, the assertion that the inductive method is scientific or objective, as supported overwhelmingly by positivists international lawyers, has received criticism from scholars of Critical Legal Study. They view this assertion as reflecting the western liberal ideological structure. Under this structure, only some arguments may be qualified as legal arguments and thus are considered, while others are ruled out of international life.[60]

Kingsbury's research on Lassa Oppenheim's positivist method of the science of law revealed that even Oppenheim's method of scientific international law incorporates political considerations to some degree.[61] Broadly speaking, Kingsbury pointed out that "Oppenheim's legal technique favored a dominant *status quo* power against a rising revisionist power."[62] Feminist approaches to international law have been more radical in criticizing the traditional international law system constructed on the basis of the effective state practice from the nineteenth century. They asserted that traditional international law is Euro-centric and androcentric, ignoring for long the feminist and the Third World perspectives in developing international legal frameworks.[63] The dominant Western conception associates with the ethics of "rule-governed adjudication of competing rights between self-interested, autonomous others."[64]

---

[60] Nigel Purvis, "Critical Legal Studies in Public International Law," *Harvard International Law Journal*, Vol. 32 (1991), p. 98.

[61] Benedict Kingsbury, "Legal Positivisim as Normative Politics: International Society, Balance of Power and Lassa Oppenheim's Positive International Law," *European Journal of International Law*, Vol. 13 (2002), p. 417 (Oppenheim's methodology for identifying rules of international law governing naval warfare was noted as prioritizing British interests in relation to attacks on foreign merchant shipping during wartime, an assessment shared by numerous commentators at the time).

[62] *Ibid.*, 417.

[63] Hilary Charlesworth, Christine Chinkin and Shelley Wright, "Feminist Approaches to International Law," *American Journal of International Law*, Vol. 85 (1991), pp. 615–617.

[64] Sandra Harding, *The Science Question in Feminism* (Cornell University Press, 1986), p. 171.

6.4 The Constructivist Critical Views on Rule-Oriented Legal Thinking and Reconsideration of Treaty Interpretation

Constructivists provide necessary broader perspectives that challenge the presumptions of a strictly rule-oriented interpretation of a treaty. Ontologically, Constructivists view treaty rules as an evolving social structure rather than merely static and regulative—actively constructive in the sense that they help to better understand the interplay between treaty rules and subsequent practice in their application, a discussion saved for the next chapter. Methodologically, Constructivists challenge positivists' views that their behaviorist approach in international relations and inductive legal methodology distort the intersubjective construction of reality. Linguistically, Constructivists adopt the position that language incorporates an indeterminate aspect. By offering critical views, particularly from methodological and linguistic view points, Constructivists help to illuminate the magic box of the treaty interpretation process and provide a deeper understanding of the riddle of treaty interpretation, though they do not resolve it entirely.

6.4.1 Constructivist's Basic Proposition

"Constructivism" is a relatively new and influential theoretical development in international relations studies.[65] Because Constructivism is still evolving in building its theoretical foundations in the study of international relations, various approaches fall under this label, making "constructivism" a less homogeneous concept.[66] No complete categorization of its sub-strains exists, although scholars have extensively explored its roots and variants.[67] Alexander Wendt grouped Constructivism as a whole with postmodern thinkers and neo-Marxists, labeling it a form of critical

[65] Professor Onuf first articulated the term "Constructivism" in the study of international relations in 1989. See Nicholas Onuf, *supra* note 15.

[66] Maja Zehfuss, "Constructivisms in International Relations: Wendt, Onuf, and Kratochwil," in K. M. Fierke and K. E. Jorgensen eds., *Constructing International Relations: The Next Generation* (M. E. Sharpe, 2001), p. 54.

[67] John G. Ruggie, "What Makes the World Hang Together? Neo-Utilitarianism and the Social Constructivist Challenge," *International Organization*, Vol. 52 (1998), pp. 857–862; John G. Ruggie, *Constructing the World Policy: Essays on International Institutionalism, II* (Routledge, 1998), p. 35 (noting the roots in the social theories of Emile Durkeim and Max Weber.). See also Jutta Brunnee and Stephen J. Toope, "International Law and Constructivism: Elements of an Interactional Theory of International Law," *Columbia Journal of Transnational Law*, Vol. 39 (2000), p. 26 (noting that the constructivist formulations have been strongly influenced by interdisciplinary studies, especially the philosophy of language and communications (Jurgen Habermas) and sociology (Anthony Giddens and Roy Bhaskar)).

theory.[68] Ted Hopf divided schools of Constructivism into "conventional" and "critical" constructivism. In Hopf's view, the two approaches share theoretical fundations but the latter is more closely aligned with critical social theory.

The vital difference between the two Constructivist approaches may exist in the areas of methodology and epistemology.[69] Precise definitions and categorizations, while important in theory building, are beyond the scope of this study. For this study, we only need to understand the basic tenets of constructivism and its interdisciplinary implications for international law. Similar to critical theorists and postmodernists, Constructivists argue that no external objective social reality exists. The key idea is that the social world, including international relations, is a human construction.[70] According to Constructivism, the materialistic foundation is not the only constituent of the world. The world is a social existence falling within an intersubjective domain: it is meaningful to the people who made it and live in it, and who understand it. It has been made or constituted by people at a particular time and place.[71]

From the Constructivists perspective on the social world as human-constructed, Constructivists challenge mainstream international relations theory both in terms of understanding of the nature of international relations and the appropriate methods for studying it. Constructivists question the plausibility of Realists propositions about the nature of political reality. They also question whether international relations can be objectively studied by using scientific methods alone. Both of these lines of inquiry carry interdisciplinary significance for international lawyers.

On the first question, Constructivists claimed that Rationalists have a blind spot regarding concepts of how the world is constructed (ontology), which leads Rationalists to believe that norms in international relations are peripheral.[72] International lawyers often share the same ontological arguments articulated by Constructivists in refuting Realists' skepticism about the role and impact of international law on states' behavior. Specifically, Constructivists contend that international law shapes interests and identities, challenging Neoliberal instrumentalism as well. However, Constructivists' critique of whether the world can be objectively discovered and explained through scientific research may make many international lawyers uneasy in their methodological approach.

---

[68] Alexander Wendt, "Constructing International Politics," *International Security*, Vol. 20 (1995), pp. 71–72.

[69] Ted Hopf, "The Promise of Constructivism in International Relations Theory," *International Security*, Vol. 23 (1998), p. 183.

[70] Robert Jackson and Georg Sorensen, *Introduction to International Relations*, (Oxford Press, 1999), p. 238. See also John G. Ruggie, "What Makes the World Hang Together? Neo-Utilitarianism and the Social Constructivist Challenge," *International Organization*, Vol. 52 (1998), p. 856 ("Constructivism is about human consciousness and its role in international life.").

[71] *Ibid.*, Robert Jackson and Georg Sorensen.

[72] Andreas Hasenclever, Peter Mayer, Volker Rittberger, *Theories of International Regimes* (Cambridge University Press, 1997), p. 23.

6.4.2 Methodological Perspective

Constructivists do not stop at merely confirming that "norms do matter" in international relations. If norms and rules matter, understanding what these specific norms and rules are, and how to properly identify them, becomes a necessary endeavor. This research agenda overlaps significantly with that of international law.

For example, in the study of regime theory, a regime is defined as "rules, norms, principles, and decision-making processes." International lawyers find that the concept of a regime closely resembles "international law by another name."[73] Some international lawyers believe the regime concept "reinvent(s) international law in rational-choice language."[74] Some even responded to the notion of a regime as "we thought of it first."[75] In regime study itself, the definitional question of what are "principles, norms, rules, and decision-making processes" was controversial when Krasner articulated the concept in 1982.[76] For Constructivists and international lawyers alike, a common core research question is how to define an international law or regime—how to properly identify one. Answering this question requires a methodological framework.

Methodological questions on how to properly identify norms and rules are closely tied to underlying ontological question about whether an objective social world exists independently of human understanding. Rationalists and Constructivists, differentiated by their divergent views on ontology, naturally engage in debate surrounding appropriate methodologies.

---

[73] Michael Byers, *Custom, Power, and the Power of Rules: International Relations and Customary International Law* (Cambridge University Press, 1998), p. 25.

[74] Anne-Marie Slaughter, "International Law and International Relations Theory," *American Journal of International Law,* Vol. 87 (1993), p. 220.

[75] Anne-Marie Slaughter, Andrew S. Tulnumello and Stepan Wood, "International Law and International Relations Theory: A New Generation of Interdisciplinary Scholarship," *American Journal of International Law*, Vol. 92 (1998), p. 378 (noting that there is a variety of international lawyers' understanding on the notion of regime). See also Shinya Murase, "Perspectives from International Economic Law on Transnational Environmental Issues", *Recueil des cours*, Vol. 253 (1995), pp. 413–414 (stating that regimes are formed on a foundation of a treaty or treaties.).

[76] Stephen D. Krasner, "Structural causes and regime consequences: regimes as intervening variables," *International Organization,* Vol. 36 (1982), p. 186. This special issue on international regimes was later published as Stephen D. Krasner, ed., *International Regimes* (Cornell University Press, 1983). Structural Realist Susan Strange criticize Krasner's definition as "imprecise and wooly." See Susan Strange, "Cave! Hic Dragones: A Critique of Regime Analysis," *International Organization,* Vol. 36 (1982), p. 479. Oran R. Young advocated for distinguishing between explicit and implicit forms of dichotomy. See Oran R. Young, *International Cooperation: Building Regimes for Natural Resources and the Environment* (Cornell University Press, 1989), p. 9. Kratochwil emphasizes "converged expectation." See Friedrich V. Kratochwil, "The Force of Prescription," *International Organization,* Vol. 38 (1984), p. 683; Friedrich V. Kratochwil and John G. Ruggie, "International Organization: A State of Art or Art of the State," *International Organization,* Vol. 40 (1986), pp. 763–764.

On methodology, Keohane advocates a Formalist approach. For Formalists, regimes can be identified through explicit rules and procedures.[77] In contrast, Young relies on observed state behavior, from which rules, norms, principles, and procedures can be inferred. Young considers that a regime can be identified where a pattern of rule-governed behavior can be observed in practice.[78] Both the Formalist and Behaviorist approach are Rationalist in orientation.[79] Behaviorists identify regimes based on observed behavior and then use the regime to "explain" the observed behavior.

Formalists view the Behaviorist approach as engaging in circular reasoning.[80] Nevertheless, Behaviorist concepts like the effectiveness of rules were incorporated into a modified Formalist approach by Keohane himself: "a regime can be identified by the existence of explicit rules that are referred to affirmatively by governments, even they are not necessarily scrupulously observed."[81] Keohane did not demand stringent effectiveness that Young did, but he did imply establishing a minimum standard. This is evident in Keohane's Rationalist taxonomy: as Rationalists view regimes as instruments in interstate cooperation, a degree of effectiveness is a requisite factor.[82]

Constructivists disagree with both the Formalist and Behaviorist methods used in identifying regimes because they overlook the normative element of regime conception—the so-called "converged expectation." A normative element forms the constitutive basis of regimes and gives them an inescapable intersubjective quality.[83] On this point, Kratochwil and Ruggie argued that "principled and shared understandings of desirable and acceptable forms of social behavior" or "element of intersubjectivity" play a central role in "knowing" regimes.[84] Failure to maintain these normative elements defeats the very purpose of regime study. In the view of Kratochwil and Ruggie, classic regime study gives rise to the problem that "epistemology fundamentally contradicts ontology."[85] Kratochwil and Ruggie urged opening up the positivist epistemology to more interpretive strains that are more closely attuned to the reality

---

[77] Keohane put forth a redefined conceptualization of regime, describing it as "Regimes are institutions with explicit rules, agreed upon by governments, that pertain to particular sets of issues in international relations." See Robert Keohane, "Neoliberal Institutionalism: A perspective on World Politics," in Robert Keohane ed., *International Institutions and State Power: Essays in International Relations Theory* (Westview Press, 1989), p. 4.

[78] Oran R. Young, *super* note 76, pp. 12–13.

[79] Andreas Hasenclever, Peter Mayer, Volker Rittberger, *Theories of International Regimes* (Cambridge University Press, 1997), p. 21.

[80] Robert Keohane, "The Analysis of International Regimes: Towards a European-American Research Programme," in Volker Rittberger ed., *Regime Theory and International Relations* (Clarendon Press, 1993), p. 27.

[81] *Ibid.*, p. 28.

[82] Robert Keohane, "International Relations and International Law: Two optics," *Harvard International Law Journal*, Vol. 38, No. 2 (Spring 1997), p. 488.

[83] Friedrich V. Kratochwil and John G. Ruggie, *super* note 76, p. 765.

[84] *Ibid.*, p. 765.

[85] *Ibid.*, p. 764.

of regimes.[86] For them, it is necessary to separate the question of the strength or effectiveness of rules and norms from the question of their existence and function.[87]

The Constructivist methodological argument has two critical points that are relevant to understanding the rules of treaties and their interpretation. First, because the argument rejects the Formalist concept of a regime (law) based soley on explicit rules and procedures, it supports the notion that the text of a treaty provides only a nominal representation of the law that has been established. Second, by rejecting the Behaviorist method for identifying a regime (law), the Constructivist methodology offers important critique of the positivist method used to identify customary rules.

6.5 Conclusion

Ambiguity in treaty provisions may be resolved by applying the general rule of interpretation codified in Article 31 of the Vienna Convention on the Law of Treaties, but this approach proves impractical for two reasons. First, the drafters of the Vienna Convention on the Law of Treaties did not adequately consider the pathology that enables ambiguity. When ambiguity results intentionally from diligent state negotiations, the ambiguous clauses seem uninterpretable since the negotiating states aimed to maintain control over discrepancies through agreed ambiguous text rather than subjecting it to interpretation. Second, the general rule of interpretation codified in Article 31 of the Vienna Convention on the Law of Treaties provides no clear guidance on obligatory method(s) for interpretation given a paradox of *Quis custodiet ipsos custodes*, and such codification is incompatible with both judicial practice and autointerpretations. For these reasons, accepting meaningful arguments by merely *invoking* Article 31 of the Vienna Convention on the Law of Treaties is very difficult.

The 1969 Vienna Convention on the Law of Treaties codified a customary textual-contextual of treaty interpretation. This "general rule of treaty interpretation" favors the textual–contextual approach. The International Law Commission's codification method to a great extent followed the English positivist legal tradition led by Oppenheim and McNair. By codifying the alleged customary rule of treaty interpretation, the International Law Commission excessively employed a positivist method in "finding" the rule of interpretation—namely, inducing the rule merely from judicial practice in treaty interpretation prior to codification at the international and domestic levels.

This method is clearly Behaviorist-oriented. Constructivists would challenge a rule codified through this methodology and reject such an inductive method, as it fails to account for the prescriptive nature of norms and rules. Applying a strictly positivist method leads to a limited and distorted understanding of norms and rules as merely regulative and static. In particular, the textual–contextual approach

[86] *Ibid.*, p. 766.

[87] Friedrih V. Kratochwil, *Rules, Norms, and Decisions: On the Conditions of Practical and Legal Reasoning in International Relations and Domestic Affairs* (Cambridge University Press, 1989), p. 46.

to treaty interpretation arises from such a constrained presumption according to Constructivists.

From the Constructivists perspective, because social reality is understood as a human construction rather than an objective phenomenon, Constructivists conclude that laws cannot be objectively discovered through scientific research or fully explained by scientific theory alone. This position forms the core of the Constructivist methodological critique of positivist approach in international law. Wendt succinctly captured this Constructivist view of methodology: "Anarchy is what states make of it."[88] The Constructivist critical methodological arguments reveal important insights about how subsequent practice should inform treaty interpretation, even if they do not directly establish a rule of interpretation. Constructivists assert the prescriptive nature of norms and rules depends on subjective elements like "shared expectation" and "intersubjective understanding" that require consideration.

Overall, Constructivism as a critical theory successfully reveals the narrow vision of mainstream international relations and international law studies regarding international norms and rules. This theory argues that international norms and rules are neither fixed by explicit wording alone nor fully discernible through state behavioral effectiveness. In the case of a treaties, Constructivists view treaty rules as not merely static and regulative but assert the positivist method leading to such constrained understandings are indeed biased and incomplete. However, the Constructivist approach still lacks a middle range theory on the mechanisms through which norms and rules emerge and evolve socially.[89] Unless the dynamics are better understood, problems of interpretation cannot be fully solved—as McDougal notes—"the determination of what text does or does not require interpretation is in itself an interpretation."[90]

---

[88] Alexander Wendt, "Anarchy Is What States Make of It," *International Organization*, Vol. 46 (1992), pp. 394–419.

[89] Jeffrey Checkel, "The Constructivist Turn in International Relations Theory," *World Politics*, Vol. 50 (1998), p. 325. Finnemore advocated initiating a research agenda centered on questions such as "How do we know a norm when we see one?," "Where do norms come from?," and "How do they change?" See Martha Finnemore and Kathryn Sikkink, "International Norm Dynamics and Political Change," *International Organization*, Vol. 52 (1998), p. 888.

[90] Myers S. McDougal, *super* note 31, p. 1023.

Chapter 7
Toward a Proper Understanding of Subsequent Practice in the Application of Dynamic Treaty Obligations

7.1 Introduction

The traditional concept of international law, or the concept of an international legal order, holds that states are subjects of international law given their relations are governed by the law that they created.[1] Because states' behavior is governed by the law, subsequent practice in the application of a treaty may give rise to disputes in its interpretation or application, often attracting analysis of whether such subsequent practice constitutes a violation. Meanwhile, subsequent practice, like any other state practice, plays an important role in shaping the rules of international law—modifying a provision of a treaty or shedding light on its interpretation.

In this chapter, I first elucidate on the features of the traditional concept of subsequent practice in the law of treaties. I seek to explain the role of subsequent practice in modern treaty law and the insufficiency of the positivist approach in addressing this area. Subsequent practice and its relevance to the application of a treaty seems not to have been fully covered in the Vienna Convention on the Law of Treaties given static views of rules and overemphasis on consent. I then aim to explicitly define a proper way to understand subsequent practice in the application of dynamic treaty obligations. The Constructivist perspectives on norms in international relations provide useful context for this purpose.

Drawing from esteemed legal theorists and leading international relations scholars, I propose a middle ground for the elaboration of the legal significance of subsequent practice in applying dynamic treaty obligations. Subsequent practice may help enhance the normativity of dynamic treaty obligations in various ways, including modification and interpretation. When evaluating subsequent practice in the application of dynamic treaty obligations, we should consider not only the degree of requisite consent but also the "extraneous rules" identifying the norm-creating character of

[1] Peter Malanczuk, *Akehurst's Modern Introduction to International Law* (7th ed. Routledge, 2002), p. 20.

X. Zhang, *Law and Politics in Peaceful Use of Nuclear Energy*,
https://doi.org/10.1007/978-981-97-3813-7_7

subsequent practices. These "extraneous rules" prove necessary in seeking a practical solution to the riddle of treaty interpretation proposed at the end of this chapter.

7.2 The Traditional Concept of Subsequent Practice in the Law of Treaties

Subsequent practice in the application of a treaty is assumed to be subject to judgment regarding violation of or compliance with a treaty. Interestingly, in this process subsequent practice also plays an important role in treaty interpretation under modern law of treaties. Meanwhile, state practice is recognized as one of the elements helping identify customary international law[2] and is highly important in developing treaty law, in that subsequent practice contributes to treaty modification.

7.2.1 The Blurred Line Between Modification and Interpretation

Modification of a treaty provision is without question a distinct law-making method compared to interpretation. In reality, subsequent practice in the application of a treaty can indeed modify its provisions. The International Law Commission considered subsequent practice a highly important topic in proposing drafts on the law of treaties, and discussions covered the subject in relation to articles on both treaty modification and treaty interpretation.

The 1964 ILC draft contained provisions concerning modification by subsequent practice and subsequent customary rules.[3] Modification by subsequent customary rule was deleted by the International Law Commission from the 1964 draft because "the question formed part of the general topic of the relation between customary norms and treaty norms which is too complex for it to be safe to deal only with one aspect of it in the present article."[4] However, modification by subsequent practice was maintained as Article 38 of the 1966 Draft.[5] In retaining this clause, the majority of the ILC members took the view that maintaining a distinction between interpretation

[2] *North Sea Continental Shelf (Federal Republic of Germany/Denmark; Federal Republic of Germany/Netherlands), Judgment,* I.C.J. Reports 1969, para. 74, p. 43.

[3] The 1964 Draft Article 68: "The operation of a treaty may also be modified ... (b): by subsequent practice in the application of the treaty establishing the agreement of the parties to modify its provisions." (c) By the subsequent emergence of a new rule of customary law relating to matters dealt with in the treaty and binding upon all the parties" See *Yearbook of the International Law Commission 1966 II*, p. 198.

[4] *Ibid.*, p. 220, p. 236. See also the comments made by the U.S delegation, *ibid.*, p. 358.

[5] *Ibid.*, p. 236.

and modification was important; they felt that keeping the rule as an independent provision was necessary.[6]

This position was repeated on several occasions in subsequent drafting. For example, when refuting "effective interpretation," the International Law Commission cited the case of the *Interpretation Peace Treaties (Advisory Opinion)* to demonstrate that "(the court) emphasized that to adopt an interpretation which ran counter to the clear meaning of the terms would not be to interpret but to revise the treaty."[7] In the ILC commentary on Article 27 of the 1966 draft (which later became Article 31 of the "General Rule of Treaty Interpretation"), the Commission referenced the *U.S. Nationals in Morocco* case and observed, "the court has more than once stressed that it is not the function of interpretation to revise or read into them what they do not expressly or by implication, contain."[8] When commenting on Article 38 of the 1966 Draft, the International Law Commission further elaborates, "[a]lthough the line may sometimes be blurred between interpretation and amendment of a treaty through subsequent practice, legally the processes are distinct."[9]

By distinguishing interpretation from modification, the International Law Commission maintained its positivist perspective in the sense that the law consists of a set of static rules. A distinction between interpretation and modification can only be drawn under the premise that the normative content of law has been fixed by a set of static rules.

When Article 38 of the 1966 Draft was submitted to states for their deliberation in the 1969 Vienna Convention on the Law of Treaties, it was rejected by a majority taking votes.[10] The direct reason for rejecting this modification method was that it seemed "redundant and to be indistinguishable from the rule of subsequent practice for interpretation."[11] Some ILC members shared this view and noticed that the subject of this rule could be covered by the rule of interpretation addressing subsequent practice, thus there was no need to keep it as an independent provision.[12]

Contemporary international judicial decisions also showed that interpretations can have the "effect of modification." In the *1963 United States v. France Air Transport Service Agreement Arbitration*, while the arbitral tribunal was asked to interpret the Air Transport Service Agreement, it concluded that the subsequent practice might in fact be viewed "as a possible source of subsequent modification."[13] Another

---

[6] *Yearbook of the International Law Commission 1966 I/2*, pp. 164–169 (See esp. Yasseen, para. 36; El-Erian, para. 44; Tunkin, para. 56; Sir Humphrey Waldock, para. 64).

[7] *Supra* note 3, p. 219.

[8] *Ibid.*, pp. 220–221.

[9] *Ibid.*, p. 236.

[10] *Ibid.*, p. 215 (53 votes to 15, with 26 abstentions).

[11] *Ibid.*, p. 300 (Comments from the Israeli Delegation on Article 68(b) of the 1964 Draft suggesting deletion).

[12] *Supra* note 6, p. 165 (See esp. Comment from Briggs on Article 68(b) of the 1964 Draft, para. 25.).

[13] *Interpretation of the Air Transport Services Agreement Between the United States (U.S.) of America and France (United States v. France) (1963)*, Reports of International Arbitral Awards, Vol. 18, pp. 62–63.

example is the ICJ's advisory opinion on the *Legal Consequences for States of the Continued Presence of South Africa in Namibia*. This case involves an interpretation of Article 27(3) of the UN Charter, which stipulates decision-making by the Security Council on all other matters requires "an affirmative vote of nine members including the concurring votes of the permanent members." While the text appears to require the five permanent members to cast affirmative votes, subsequent Council voting practice took "concurring" to mean not to cast a "veto," such that abstention or even absence did not prevent a resolution's adoption. An example of such an interpretive practice was the Soviet Union absence in the Council's decision on taking actions in the Korean War in 1950. In the instant advisory opinion, the ICJ upheld an interpretation of Article 27(3) based on such a subsequent practice.[14] However, it was observed that the *travaux préparatoires* of the Charter contained no evidence of such an intention among the permanent members.[15]

Ultimately, by adopting articles of the Vienna Convention on the Law of Treaties, states chose to address subsequent practice in the application of a treaty within the rule of treaty interpretation rather than the rule of treaty modification. While some ILC members explained that overlapping rules of interpretation and modification prevented addressing the same subject matter twice in the law of treaties, this does not explain the preference for the rule of interpretation over modification. A priority seems to have existed when considering how to handle subsequent practice within the legal framework.

By opting for the rule on interpretation to address subsequent practice, states demonstrated their understanding of the dynamic nature of treaty rules and the appropriate role of subsequent practice in applying a treaty comprising dynamic obligations. The boundary between interpretation and modification through subsequent practice was not distinctly demarcated.[16] Drawing such a distinction is no longer necessary, if not impossible, because modification can only occur when the prior rule is clear. Otherwise, everything becomes a matter of interpretation since norms are continually evolving. Regarding the blurred boundary between modification and interpretation, states suggest adopting a different theoretical perspective beyond

[14] *Legal Consequences for States of the Continued Presence of South Africa in NamibiaLegal Consequences for States of the Continued Presence of South Africa in Namibia (South West Africa) notwithstanding Security Council Security Council Resolution 276 (1970), Advisory Opinion,* I.C.J. Reports 1971, p. 22, para. 22.

[15] Leland M. Goodrich, Edvard Hambro and Anne Patricia Simons, *Charter of the United Nations: Commentary and Documents* (Columbia University Press, 1969), p. 229.

[16] Some international lawyers insisted that the distinction was necessary and claimed that though it failed in codification, the rule of modification by subsequent practice was still a customary rule. See N. Kontou, *The Termination and Revision of Treaties in the Light of New Customary International Law* (Clarendon Press, 1994), p. 27; P. Reuter, *Introduction to the Law of Treaties* (Pinter Publishers, 1989), p. 159; Maek. E. Villiger, *Customary International Law and Treaties: A Manual on the Theory and Practice of the Interrelation of Sources* (2nd ed. Kluwer Law International, 1997), p. 211. See also *Yearbook of the International Law Commission, 1966 II*, pp. 164–169, pp. 220–221 (International Law Commission members' opinion on the customary nature of this rule), p. 358 (The U.S. regarded the provision as reflecting long-standing and wide accepted practice).

strict positivism: norms are in a constant state of flux, so the delineation between modification and interpretation is scarcely discernable.

7.2.2 *Subsequent Practice and Interpretation: Treaty-Oriented and Customary Practice*

In the Vienna Convention on the Law of Treaties, as a constituent part of the general customary of interpretation, Article 31(3) stipulates:

> ...(b) any subsequent practice in the application of the treaty which establishes the agreement of the parties regarding its interpretation and
>
> (c) any relevant rules of international law applicable in the relations between the parties.

Subsequent practice in 31(3)(b) is a "treaty-oriented practice." According to the ILC commentary, "the agreement of the parties" means an agreement that can be established by the parties as a whole. However, not every party is required to engage individually in the practice. Acceptence by every party is sufficient in establishing such an agreement.[17] Further, subsequent practice must be "consistent" and must "establish parties' understanding regarding the meaning of the provisions of the treaty."[18]

In case law, a significant variety of subsequent practices exist. Subsequent practices could be a "consistent course of conduct,"[19] "consistently and uniformly interpreted the practice,"[20] a one-time practice in interpreting a bilateral treaty,[21] or a subsequent memorandum of understanding (MOU) constituting "consensual subsequent practice by the parties."[22]

The variety of subsequent practices seen in case law does little to establish criteria for judging the necessary degree of consistency or uniformity required to demonstrate "an agreement" and verify "subsequent practice in the application of the treaty." For

---

[17] *Supra* note 3, p. 222.

[18] *Supra* note 3, 236. See also Sinclair, *The Vienna Convention on the Law of Treaties* (Manchester University Press, 1973), p. 138. (Sinclair believed that Article 31(3)(b) "does not cover subsequent practice in general but only a specific form of subsequent practice—that is to say, concordant subsequent practice common to all the parties.").

[19] *The Chamizal Case (Mexico, United States) (1911)*, Reports of International Arbitral Awards, Vol. 6, p. 338.

[20] *Supra* note 14.

[21] *Case concerning the Temple of Preah Vihear (Cambodia v. Thailand), Merits, Judgment of 15 June 1962*, I.C.J. Reports 1962, pp. 33–34 (The Court accepted the map-line in practice for determining a portion of the boundary in the temple area as evidence of authentic interpretation, and this practice will prevail over the treaty clause. The reason was that the map had been accepted by the Thai government regardless of the fact that Thailand only dispatched low-ranking officials in handling the map business. The treaty rule was not modified because in the other portions of the boundary, the watershed-line rule in the treaty remained applicable).

[22] *United States-United Kingdom Arbitration concerning Heathrow Airport User Charges (United States-United Kingdom) (1994)*, Reports of International Arbitral Awards, Vol. 24, paras. 6.7, p. 131.

example, in the case of a multilateral treaty, how many parties need to be signatories to a MOU for its interpretation of that treaty to constitute a subsequent practice?

To address such questions requires understanding what legally constitutes subsequent practice in interpretation. The International Law Commission indicated that "the agreement of the parties" could be explained in terms of their consent[23] and that the agreement denotes "tacit agreement."[24] Reuter noted that treaty-oriented practice "amounted to a tacit agreement rather than to a custom."[25] Kontou also believes speaking of treaty modification (by subsequent practice) by implied consent is more appropriate, as this practice is treaty-oriented and motivated by intent to modify the conventional norm rather than create exceptions to general custom. This type of practice does not independently establish special customs without separate proof of *opinio juris*.[26]

From these arguments, we can infer that subjective elements exist in the consent or implied consent achieved through subsequent practice in the application of a treaty. Under Article 2(1) (a) of the Vienna Convention on the Law of Treaties, a treaty is defined as instruments "governed by international law." According to the ILC commentary, this implies treaties incorporate an intention to generate obligations under international law.[27] Therefore, subsequent practice carried out "in the application of the treaty" necessarily involves this subjective element by association.

An important distinction exists between the two types of subsequent practice provided in Article 31(3) (b) and (c). The former constitutes a "treaty-oriented practice" linked to the intention of the States Party to create obligations under international law. The latter presents a "customary rule-oriented" practice irrelevant to states' intention concerning a treaty. Applying a customary rule-oriented practice in treaty interpretation seems to necessitate separate proof of *opinio juris* in evaluating the subsequent practice legally pertinent to the interpretation process.

Nevertheless, can *opinio juris* relevant to states' intention in a treaty be adopted as an independent legal foundation when assessing the legal significance of a treaty's interpretation? Akehurst noted,

> What counts is the practice followed *inter se* by the parties to the treaty; the practice which they follow in their dealing with States which are not parties to the treaty, and the practice of the latter states, may give rise to a rule of customary rule, but such rule has no effect on the treaty unless it is followed by the parties to the treaty in their relations with one another.[28]

Kontou believed *opinio juris* review was unnecessary for evaluating a treaty's rights and obligations.[29] She argued a new rule of customary law binding all states

---

[23] *Yearbook of the International Law Commission, 1964 II*, p. 198; *Yearbook of the International Law Commission, 1966 II*, p. 236.

[24] *Yearbook of the International Law Commission, 1966 I/2*, pp. 221–222.

[25] Paul Reuter, *supra* note 16, p. 138.

[26] N. Kontou, *supra* note 16, pp. 27–28.

[27] *Supra* note 3, 189.

[28] Michael. Akehurst, "The Hierarchy of the Sources of International Law", *British Yearbook of International Law*, Vol. 47 (1974–1975), p. 276.

[29] N. Kontou, *supra* note 16, p. 30.

parties could not automatically terminate a treaty rule without clear intent to terminate or modify the treaty.[30] In conflicts, treaty rules must be applied as they stand.[31] Following this logic, using subsequent "customary rule-oriented" practice in treaty interpretation is constrained. However, Kontou also suggested a constructive way to understand custom's role in treaty interpretation. In her view, treaty-making cannot occur without customary law as "legal background" having "logical priority."[32] When customary law changes, contracting relations based on the prior legal regime embedded with old custom require reassessment and fresh interpretation.[33]

If distinguishing the role of subsequent practice in treaty interpretation from modification is impossible, then distinguishing treaty-oriented from customary-oriented subsequent practice lacks meaning, as both may constitute the consent required for interpretation under modern treaty law. Nuance only exists in theory regarding subjective elements of the consent. The former connects to states parties' intent to create obligations related to the interpreted treaty; the latter relies on independent *opinio juris*. However, as Sinclair correctly noted, "customary rule-oriented" practice "[can] be taken into account in interpreting certain terms which are by their very nature expressed in such general terms as to lend themselves to an evolutionary interpretation."[34]

In summary, the traditional concept of subsequent practice in the application of a treaty is strongly associated with positivist, rule-oriented legal thinking wherein international law comprises a set of rules. Subsequent practice is then subject to modification or interpretation rules. The codified general rule of treaty interpretation in the 1969 Vienna Convention on the Law of Treaties views treaty provisions as static—meaning is fixed at adoption. Treaty rules thus determined are regulative in that subsequent practice, through employing the general rule of interpretation, ultimately faces a legal–illegal judgment backed by sanctions[35] derived from a grundnorm[36] or rule of recognition.[37]

This discussion ultimately returns to the Hart-D'Amato' understanding of international obligation—"An obligation arises because states *say* that they have undertaken it and international law exists because states and people believe and say so"[38]

[30] *Ibid.*, 29.

[31] *Ibid.*, 19. Hersch Lauterpacht, *The Development of International Law by the International Court* (London: Stevens & Sons, Ltd.; New York: Frederick A. Praeger, 1958), p. 155. et seq.

[32] N. Kontou, *supra* note 16, p. 157.

[33] *Ibid.*, p.157.

[34] Ian Sinclair, *supra* note 18, p. 140.

[35] John Austin, *Lectures On Jurisprudence* (Thoemmes Press, 1996).

[36] See in general Hans Kelsen, *General Theory of Law and State* (Harvard University Press, 1949).

[37] See in general H. L. A. Hart, *The Concept of Law* (rev. ed. Clarendon Press 1961), p. 89, p. 96; H. L. A. Hart, *Essays in Jurisprudence and Philosophy* (Clarendon Press, 1983).

[38] Dencho Georgiev, "Politics or Rule of Law: Deconstruction and Legitimacy in International Law," *European Journal of International Law,* Vol. 4 (1993), p. 5.

(emphasis added). While some appraised it as magical[39] others critiqued this definition of a legal obligation as entirely circular.[40] The Hartian interpretive approach and circular reasoning are perhaps best exemplified in Article 31(3) (b) and (c), which prescribe treaty interpretation by subsequent practice while futilely seeking party agreement for clear obligation prescription.

Is this rule-oriented legal thinking adequate for understanding subsequent practice in interpreting or applying dynamic treaty obligations? In modern law of treaties, subsequent practice is viewed narrowly as just one interpretive element, which fails to capture its actual modification role. As discussed, agreement on authentic interpretation through subsequent practice seems illusory given real-world realities. All of this indicates subsequent practice is not sufficiently addressed in modern law of treaties.

7.3 Insufficiency of Rule-Oriented Legal Thinking and the Problems of Subsequent Practice

In the following section, I will explore the debate between Rationalists and Constructivists in the study of international relations and consider implications for rethinking traditional, rule-oriented treaty interpretation. A static, regulatory perspective on norms and rules reveals some aspects of reality but not the full picture. In treaty interpretation, ambiguous language drafted intentionally by negotiators challenges narrow, static assumptions. Reexamining presumptions when seeking interpretive rules becomes prudent.

7.3.1 The Constructivists' Contribution: The Ontological Perspective

Constructivists presume the world consists not just of material forces but also of "intersubjective" dimensions beyond reduction to individual actors. Norms and rules should no longer be viewed solely as static entities with only a regulatory function. Rather, they are constitutive in nature, and the constructive interplay between norms and interests is best understood through the constructivist lens of norms and rules as dynamic entities.

Constructivists view the social structure as including international norms and institutions, illustrating the legacy of regime studies.[41] Robert Keohane later categorized

---

[39] *Ibid.*, p. 5.

[40] Martha Finnemore and Stephen J Toope, "Alternatives to 'Legalization': Richer Views of Law and Politics," *International Organization,* Vol. 55 (Summer 2001), p. 743.

[41] The status of international rules in international relations has long been a key topic in the study of both International Relations (IR) and International Law (IL). The debate can be traced back to the

institutional studies into rationalist and the reflective (constructivist) approaches.[42] Generally, Rationalists assert that "behavior can be adjudged objectively to be optimally adapted to the situation."[43] For Rationalists, states "are rational when they choose strategies that they believe will have the optimal consequences given their interests. The expected costs and benefits of different choices are compared, and the one with the highest net value is chosen."[44] Constructivists' ontological perspective does not assume states possess rational capacity to calculate interests or maximize utility. Rather, Classical and Structural Realists, and Neo-liberalists as well, shared Rationalists' portrayal of states as self-interested actors in international relations.

For Rationalists, state behavior can be evaluated by the extent to which it maximizes individual utility. Classical and Structural Realists seek absolute or positional power maximization,[45] while Neoliberalists focuses on cooperative interests.[46] All three schools embrace rationalism[47] —viewing norms and rules in regimes are determined solely by material factors relating to states' static, self-interested power and

moralist (legalist)-realist debate in the U.S. foreign policy making that started in the period between the two Great Wars of the last century, when realist thinking led by Professor Morgenthau and Mr. George Kennan dominated U.S. foreign policy. The revival of the study of norms and rules in IR is evidenced by the emergence of regime theory in the early 1980s. Krasner rendered the oft-cited definition of regime as "sets of implicit or explicit principles, norms, rules, and decision-making procedures around which actors' expectations converge in a given area of international relations." See Stephen D. Krasner, "Structural causes and regime consequences: regimes as intervening variables," *International Organization,* Vol. 36 (1982), p. 186. This special issue on international regimes was later published as Stephen D. Krasner, ed., *International Regimes* (Cornell University Press, 1983). Various approaches have been employed in the study of regime, and consequently, each tended to use terms from their own discipline such as "institution" (more often used by sociologist), "norm" (political science), "rule" (international law). See Finnemore, "International Norm Dynamics and Political Change," *International Organization,* Vol. 52 (1998), p. 891.

42 Robert Keohane, "International Institutions: Two Approaches," *International Studies Quarterly,* Vol. 32 (1988), pp. 379–396 (Keohane used "reflective approaches" instead of constructivist approaches. However, the two terms are interchangeable).

43 Herbert A. Simon, "Human Nature in Politics: The Dialogue of Psychology with Political Science," *American Political Science Review,* Vol. 79 (1985), p. 294.

44 Alexander Wendt, "Driving with the Rearview Mirror: On the Rational Science of Institutional Design," *International Organization,* Vol. 55 (2001), p. 1023.

45 Miles Kahler, "Rationality in International Relations," *International Organization,* Vol. 52 (1998), p. 920, pp. 923–925 (noting that Realism's relationship with Rationalist theory has been uneasy, and rationality assumption is one of three key assumptions that define the "hard core" of the realist research program). See also Joseph M. Grieco, "Anarchy and the Limits of Cooperation: A Realist Critique of the Newest Liberal Institutionalism," *International Organization,* Vol. 42 (1988), p. 488 (explaining the realist proposition related to rationalism).

46 *Ibid.*, Joseph M. Grieco, p. 492 (noting that neoliberals shared the realist assumption that states are unitary-rational agents). Robert Keohane, *After Hegemony: Cooperation and Discord in the World Political Economy* (Princeton University Press, 1984), p. 27 (noting the difference between the two approaches is whether states as rational agents are egoistic (Neoliberalism) or positional (Neorealism)). See also John J. Mearsheimer, "The False Promise of International Institutions," *International Security,* Vol. 19 (1995), p. 11; Kenneth Waltz, *Theory of International Politics* (McGraw-Hill, 1979), p. 126.

47 Andreas Hasenclever, Peter Mayer, Volker Rittberger, *Theories of International Regimes* (Cambridge University Press, 1997), p. 23; Robert Keohane, *supra* note 42, p. 381.

welfare calculations, and do not have their own lives. Sanctions, inducements, and other means Rationalists see as sustaining regimes rely on a fixed set of regulatory rules governing states behavior.

Constructivists fundamentally differ from Rationalists in their ontological approach.[48] They critique Rationalists as being purely materialistic with an individualistic world view that fails to acknowledge the social dimensions of structures.[49] Constructivists assert social structures contain "shared knowledge, material resources, and practices"[50]that imbue material factors with meaning.[51]

To illustrate, Wendt cited the security dilemma, noting "500 British nuclear weapons are less threatening to the United States than 5 North Korean nuclear weapons, because the British are friends of the United States and the North Koreans are not, and amity or enmity is a function of shared understandings."[52] For Wendt, social reality cannot be positively detected by measuring solely material factors like military or ecnomic power. Material factors only have meaning when integrated through interactions in an intersubjective social structure.

At the ontological level, Constructivists conclude that the nature of international relations is a social construction. Norms and institutions should not be viewed merely as a reflection of power dynamic and interest calculations. Further, Constructivists posits agents (states) and structures (norms) are mutually constitutive entities with equal ontological status.[53] In this view, international norms and institutions, like material forces, have lives of their own and "do matter" independently in shaping international relations.

48 John G. Ruggie, "What Makes the World Hang Together? Neo-Utilitarianism and the Social Constructivist Challenge," *International Organization*, Vol. 52 (1998), p. 879 (noting that the most distinctive feature of constructivism is in the realm of ontology).

49 Andreas Hasenclever, Peter Mayer, *supra* note 47, pp. 158–161.

50 Alexander Wendt, "Constructing International Politics," *International Security*, Vol. 2 (1995), p. 73.

51 *Ibid*., p. 73.

52 *Ibid*., p. 73.

53 Alexander Wendt, "The Agent Structure Problem in International Relation Theory," *International Organization*, Vol. 41 (1987), p. 339.

Constructivists also argue norms and rules are not merely regulative but also constitutive in nature.[54] By stressing norms and rules' constitutive quality, constructivism reject the notion that they are fixed and static. In contrast, norms and rules are viewed as dynamic processes within the social construction. Nothing is given or certain, everything is seen as intersubjective and in flux within the ongoing construction of the social structure.

In conclusion, Constructivism's ontological framework provides an alternative understanding of the nature of international norms, rules, and law. No longer viewed merely through an "instrumentalist" lens, international law is posited to independently "matter" in shaping international relations.[55] This challenges Realists' instrumentalist understanding of international law and allies constructivism with international legal scholars.[56]

More importantly, Constructivism posits international law matters in ways beyond mere regulation. This view helps liberate international lawyers from an overstated legal positivist understanding of law as solely comprising static rules. Constructivism's ontological framework supports asserting treaty rules as a social structure are always evolving through interaction between agents and structures within intersubjective processes of social construction.

[54] Finnemore and Kratochivil distinguished regulative rules from constitutive rules, viewing regulative rules as the only module of rationalists. See Finnemore, *supra* note 41, p. 891; Martha Finnemore, "Are Legal Norms Distinctive?" *New York University Journal of International Law and Politics,* Vol. 32 (2000), p. 702; Frederich Kratochwil, "How Do Norms Matter," in Michael Byers ed., *The Role of Law in International Politics* (Oxford University Press, 2000), pp. 56–57; Friedrih V Kratochwil, *Rules, Norms, and Decisions: On the Conditions of Practical and Legal Reasoning in International Relations and Domestic Affairs* (Cambridge University Press, 1989), p. 28. On the other hand, Onuf, relying on Giddens' theory, rejected the view that there are separate regulative rules and constitutive rules, arguing that regulative rules are at the same time constructive. He claims: "Social order cannot be systematically derived from individual maximizing choice." See Nicholas Onuf, "The Constitution of international politics" *European Journal of International Law,* Vol. 5 (1994), p. 7.

[55] Robert Keohane, "International Relations and International Law: Two optics," *Harvard International Law Journal,* Vol. 38 (1997), pp. 498–99. Slaughter also claimed "functionalists has rediscovered of international law in regimes but refuse to recognize the very nature of it." See Anne-Marie Slaughter "International Law and International Relations Theory," *American Journal of International Law,* Vol. 87 (1993), pp. 219–220.

[56] Anthony Clark Arend, "Toward understanding of International Legal Rules," in Robert Beck, Anthony Arend, and Robert Vander Lugt eds., *International Rules: Approaches from International Law and International Relations* (Oxford University Press, 1996), p. 290 (viewing law as a set of rules but not process). However, he applied Constructivist ontological argument as a theoretical foundation for understanding international politics. See Anthony Clark Arend, *Legal Rules and International Society* (Oxford University Press, 1999), p. 148.

7.3.2 Subsequent Practice in "Interpreting" Dynamic Obligations and Legal Theories

Constructivism supports the key proposition that international law should be viewed not as static rules but as a dynamic social process. Accordingly law no longer merely constrains through legal–illegal judgments. Treaties equally comprise an evolving process of social construction lacking certainty.[57] This perspective informed the ILC's view that subsequent practice may constitute an "authentic interpretation" of a treaty subject to conditions.[58] Constructivism posits states consent to treaties based not only on material interests but also normative appropriateness, with social norms influencing decision making.

While acknowledging social construction, it bears noting consent remains central to international law making given today's world system is made of sovereign states.[59] State sovereignty, from the Hobbesian roots,[60] implies the traditional consent doctrine that states are not subject to any rules except those they agreed to.[61] International law is thus no more than the rules to which states have agreed to through treaties, custom, and perhaps other forms of consent[62]—states' consent becomes formal source of international law.[63]

---

[57] In the *Barcelona Traction* case, the ICJ stated that treaty rules, as part of the social structure, will not live in a vacuum but keep evolving. See, *Barcelona Traction, Light and Power Company, Limited, Judgment*, I.C.J. Reports 1970, p. 33, para. 37.

[58] Sir Humphrey Waldock, one of the Special Rapporteurs of the International Law Commission on the law of treaties, saw subsequent practice as "an authentic interpretation comparable to interpretative agreement." See *Yearbook of the International Law Commission 1966 II*, p. 98.

[59] Leo Gross, "The Peace of Westphalia: 1648–1948," *American Journal of International Law*, Vol. 42 (1948), pp. 2041 (discussing the emergence of sovereign states in Europe and the Peace of Westphalia of 1648).

[60] Ulrich Fastenrath, "Relative Normativity in International Law," *European Journal of International Law*, Vol. 4 (1993), pp. 305–340 (discussing the origin of Voluntarism from the tradition of Hobbes); Edwin Smith, "Understanding Dynamic Obligations: Arms Control Agreements," *South California Law Review*, Vol. 64 (1990–1991), pp. 1567–1568 (discussing the problem of Hobbesian understanding of law).

[61] James L. Brierly, *The Law of Nations* (Oxford, 1963), pp. 7–16, pp. 51–52. Robert Y. Jennings and Sir Arthur Watts, *Oppenheim's International Law*, Vol. I (9th ed. Longman, 1992), pp. 14–16. In the *Lotus* case the Permanent Court of International Justice stated: "International law governs relations between independent states. The rules of law binding upon states therefore emanate from their own free will as expressed in conventions or by usages generally accepted as expressing principles of law." See *The Case of the S. S. "Lotus" (France v. Turkey), Judgment,* 1927 P.C.I.J. (Series A), No. 10, p. 19. International Court of Justice in the *Military and Paramilitary Activities in and Against Nicaragua* case stated "In international law there are no rules, other than such rules as may be accepted by the states concerned...whereby the level of armaments of a sovereign State can be limited." See *Military and Paramilitary Activities in and Against Nicaragua (Nicaragua v. United States), Merits, Judgment,* I.C.J. Reports 1986, p. 135, para. 269.

[62] Robert W. Tucker rev. and ed., Hans Kelsen, *Principles of International Law* (2nd ed. Holt, Rinehart & Winston, 1966), pp. 438–439.

[63] P. E. Corbett, "The Consent of States and the Source of the Law of Nations," *British Yearbook of International Law*, Vol. 6 (1925), pp. 23–30. An extreme form of this Hobbesian root of voluntarism

However, constructivism suggests restricting analysis to a Hobbesian view of states as individualistic actors pursuing solely self-interest is unnecessary. In constructing the present world of sovereign states, constructivism posits underlying constitutive norms exist that define sovereignty itself. Even in an extreme form of international society, for instance anarchy, the rule of sovereignty operates to construct anarchy.[64]

Overall, while consent remains necessary, constructivism suggests it is not alone sufficient to understand evolving international legal obligations. Using consent as the sole foundation fails to explain how obligations can persist beyond an initial consent.[65] Fitzmaurice suggested an alternative view:

> [Consent] is a *method* of creating rules, but it is not, in the last resort, the element that makes the rules binding, when created. In short, consent could not, in itself, create obligations unless there were already in existence a rule of law according to which consent had just that effect[66] (italics in the original).

The debate around consent's role as the basis versus method of international legal obligation echoes a familiar discussion between the authoritative power of sovereign consent and the possibility of extraconsensual norms developing over time.

Fitzmaurice argued that consent alone cannot produce bindingness, and is not the sole means by which legal rules emerge. Consent relies on an extraneous validating rule—having force irrespective of consent.[67] Examples include *pacta sunt servanda*. While traditionally pairing consent and *pacta sunt servanda* establishes treaties as the obligation's basis, this leads to formalism and inflexibility at odds with the lived, evolving nature of legal systems.

Certain legal theories similarly reject consent alone sufficient for legal obligation. Hart proposed extraconsensual norms (secondary rules) as the basis of the obligation with rules comprising primary norms.[68] Following Hart, D'Amato argued states had accepted secondary rules through "consensus" in legal argumentation

---

approach to international law can be seen in the fact that in the Soviet international law theory, treaty and custom are no difference in deed because the consent requirement in custom formation is no less flexible than the treaty's—custom became legally binding only when so agreed by the States. See Robert Y. Jennings and Sir Arthur Watts, *supra* note 61, pp. 14–16.

64 Kenneth W. Abbott, Robert O. Keohane, Andrew Moravcsik, Anne-Marie Slaughter, and Duncan Snidal, "The Concept of Legalization," *International Organization*, Vol. 54 (2000), p. 407.

65 Edwin Smith, *supra* note 60, p. 1567.

66 Gerald Fitzmaurice, "The Foundations of the Authority of International Law and the Problem of Enforcement," *Modern Law Review*, Vol. 19 (1956), p. 9, cited in Michael Byers, *Custom, Power, and the Power of Rules: International Relations and Customary International Law* (Cambridge University Press, 1998), p. 8.

67 Sir Gerald Fitzmaurice, "Some Problems Regarding the Formal Sources of International Law," *Symbolae Verzijl* (The Hague 1958), p. 167–168. His reasoning was that, if there is a rule (call it Rule X) that general consent, assent, acquiescence or recognition in some form is invariably necessary before a given rule (Rule X1) is binding or has the force of law, what gave the basic rule (X) its legal force or made it binding? To say consent would merely be to argue in a circle and to attempt to prove a proposition in terms of itself.

68 H. L. A. Hart, *The Concept of Law* (Clarendon Press, 1961), p. 92, pp. 208–231.

relying on primary rules of international law.[69] Relatedly, work on "The Concept of Legalization" defined that "legal obligations bring into play the established norms, procedures, and forms of discourse of the international legal system."[70] While helpfully rectifying formalistic understandings of consent, these theories still characterize treaty rules statically rather than as constitutively constructed.[71]

The notion of "dynamic obligation" considers treaty rules as an ongoing process, not an immutable outcome, with their construction continually influenced by consensual means. Two points need to be clarified in discussing interpretive problems. First, viewing the law as a process precludes distinguishing treaty interpretation from modification, as confirmed by international judicial practice discussed in the preceding section. Second, if subsequent practice in elucidating dynamic obligations carries the same law-making import as consent or "extraneous rules," both sources must factor into relevance determinations for practices guiding interpretation. However, which specific practices are legally germane was an issue raised previously yet still awaiting resolution.

Even as the Vienna Convention on the Law of Treaties was negotiated, Professor McDougal of the U.S. Delegation criticized its excessive emphasis on a textual–contextual approach in treaty interpretation.[72] McDougal and his New Haven School (NHS) associates were eloquent proponents of viewing "law as a process".[73] For the New Haven School, law making must consider extraneous factors such as "authoritative decision making" or "human dignity." Thus, they advocated treaty interpretation should aim to ascertain "the genuine shared principles of the parties,"[74] priorities "the overriding objectives of human dignity" and "fundamental community policy," with the latter able to supersede contractual expectations in cases of grave contradiction.[75]

The New Haven School differs from the traditional rule-oriented legal thinking in emphasizing process over static rules seen as merely regulative. It questions the

---

[69] Anthony A. D'Amato, *The Concept of Custom in International Law* (Cornell University Press, 1971), pp. 41–44, p. 191.

[70] Kenneth W. Abbott, Robert O. Keohane, Andrew Moravcsik, Anne-Marie Slaughter, and Duncan Snidal, *supra* note 64, p. 409.

[71] Edwin Smith, *supra* note 60, p. 1571 (Smith's understanding of Hart's obligation is similar to D'Amato. He wrote: "Obligations exist to the extent that states judge themselves by those obligations: to the extent that states justify and criticize their actions in terms of international legal rules.").

[72] Myers S. McDougal, "Statement of Professor Myers S. McDougal, United States Delegation, to Committee of the Whole, April 19, 1968," *American Journal of International Law*, Vol. 62 (1968), pp. 1021–1027.

[73] Myers S. McDougal, "International Law, Power and Policy: A Contemporary Conception," *Recueil des Cours*, Vol. 82 (1953), pp. 182–183; Myers S. McDougal, "Law as a Process of Decision: A Policy-Oriented Approach to Legal Study," *Natural Law Forum*, Vol. 1 (1956), p. 53; Myers S. McDougal and Harold D. Lasswell, "The Identification and Appraisal of Drivers Systems of Public Order," *American Journal of International Law*, Vol. 53 (1959), pp. 1–29.

[74] Myres S. McDougal, Harold D. Lasswell and James C. Miller, *The Interpretation of Agreement and World Public Order: Principles of Content and Procedure* (Yale University Press, 1967), p. 22.

[75] *Ibid*, pp. 40–41.

usefulness of conceptualizing rules in this constrained manner.[76] Additionally, the School rejects the notion that a rule's constraining force stems from hierarchical validation within a system. Instead, they assert binding nature arises from a rule's effectiveness in advancing communal objectives.

Jutta Brunnee and Stephen Toope concurred with the New Haven School's conceptualization of law as a process. However, Toope critiqued an essential flaw of the New Haven School—its potential drift toward raw instrumentalism. Specifically, an assumption of universal agreement on liberal democracy's moral high ground and willingness to use compulsion to propagate such values globally.[77] This risk of overreach retains an undertone of strong hegemony at odds with the School's aims of collaborative and inclusive scholarship.[78]

Brunnee and Toope cited Lon Fuller's description of law as "a potentially beautiful but inevitably incomplete construction that is best viewed as a continuing challenge rather than as a finished project."[79] They draw from Fuller's concept of "internal morality" as an extraconsensual element ensuring legal binding-ness.[80] Fuller posited eight such requirements: generality of rules; promulgation; limiting cases of retroactivity; clarity; avoidance of contradiction; not asking the impossible; consistency over time; and congruence of official action with the underlying rules. For Fuller, law is recognizable through adherence to these requirements of "internal morality."[81] Thomas Franck similarly suggested legitimacy relies on promulgation, limiting cases of retroactivity, clarity, and avoiding secrecy.[82] These extraconsensual elements could strengthen an imperfect agreement among states via enhanced adherence generated though their subsequent practice. They thus aid interpreting treaties by illuminating subsequent practice's role regarding the mysterious "agreement of the parties regarding its interpretation."

Brunnee and Toope further asserted that normativity arises through the pervasive interaction of ends and means. For legitimacy, norms must also withstand external valuations like equality, transparency, justice, and fairness testing.[83] Brunnee and Toope emphasized Fuller's "internal morality" focus on creation, interpretation and administration processes distinguished his neutral, non-natural law theory from prior

---

[76] Myres McDougal and Harold Lasswell, *supra* note 73, pp. 1–12.

[77] Stephen Toope, "Emerging Patterns of Governance," in Michael Byers ed., *The Role of Law in International Politics* (Oxford University Press, 2000), pp. 100–101.

[78] *Ibid.*, p. 93.

[79] Jutta Brunnee and Stephen J. Toope, "International Law and Constructivism: Elements of an Interactional Theory of International Law," *Columbia Journal of Transnational Law*, Vol. 39 (2000), p. 45. For Fuller's description of law, see Lon L. Fuller, *The Morality of Law* (Yale University Press, 1969), p. 106, p. 145.

[80] Jutta Brunnee and Stephen J. Toope, *ibid.*, p. 56.

[81] Jutta Brunnee and Stephen J. Toope, "The Changing Nile Basin Regime: Does Law Matter?" *Harvard International Law Journal,* Vol. 43 (2002), p. 115.

[82] Thomas Franck, *The Power of Legitimacy among Nations* (Oxford University Press, 1990), p. 49 (Four variables affecting legitimacy: determinacy, symbolic validation, coherence, and adherence).

[83] Jutta Brunnee and Stephen J. Toope, "Environmental Security and Freshwater Resources: Ecosystem Regime Building," *American Journal of International Law*, Vol. 92 (1997), p. 32.

traditions.[84] Fuller's interactional understanding of law, stressing mutuality between the governing and the governed, precludes social control solely by rules.[85]

While relying on Fuller's theory and Constructivism, Jutta Brunnee and Stephen J. Toope suggested reexamining the consensual fiction of international law. However, two key issues seem to remain open for discussion. First, their framework appears to overlook consent entirely as a lawmaking method,[86] relying solely on internal characteristics to determine bindingness[87]—conflicting with sovereign states' role in consent-based law creation. Second, empirically applying "internal morality" tests, admittedly, "are not perfect and other formulations would be plausible."[88]

Nevertheless, Lon Fuller's interactional legal theory helps evaluate the legal relevance of subsequent practice to treaty interpretation by emphasizing mutual shaping between those governing and governed. This suggests agreements among the governed hold particular importance. His framework usefully breaks the circular reasoning around Article 31(3)(b)'s "parties' agreement" concept, which currently lacks independent extra-consensual criteria for establishing "agreement of the parties regarding its interpretation."

7.3.3 A Practical Solution: Subsequent Practice and Good Faith in Treaty Interpretation

Article 31(3) (b) on treaty interpretation by subsequent practice limits relying on consent alone. Theories like Critical Legal Study and New Haven School suggest focusing more on normative content than strict wording,[89] indicating extra-consensual elements are needed alongside consent in assessing subsequent practice's legal relevance to the "agreement of the Parties regarding its interpretation." Drawing on these perspectives, a practical solution could involve introducing extra-legal criteria for properly comprehending the relationship between evolving practice and living treaty interpretation over time.

The search for a resolution begins by asking questions. If the paradox of *Quis custodiet ipsos custodes* renders treaty interpretation mythical under the current rule, could guidance exist outside this framework? If none can be found, does that imply interpretation faces no constraints in international law? What reality does the general rule of interpretation (Article 31) reflect regarding the nature of the task?

---

[84] Jutta Brunnee and Stephen J. Toope, *super* note 79, p. 56.

[85] *Ibid.*, p. 49.

[86] *Ibid.*, p. 56 ("If the internal morality of the law is not fulfilled, if the conditions are not met, then the process of law creation, be it through legislation, adjudication or negotiation, is fundamentally flawed and therefore illegitimate.").

[87] Jutta Brunnee and Stephen J. Toope, *super* note 81, pp. 115–116.

[88] *Ibid.*, 115.

[89] Ulrich Fastenrath, *super* note 60, p. 311.

One potential approach may involve seeking the rule of interpretation in customary international law,[90] given general acceptance of such a rule's customary status.[91] However, customary rules are notoriously unclear and indeterminate. As evidenced even by the International Law Commission's efforts to codify previously customary principle of treaty interpretation, identifying precise customary content in practice proves difficult. While a customary rule of treaty interpretation theoretically exists, uncertainty surrounds discerning its specific normative contours.[92]

Some may propose applying principles or techniques used in domestic contract or statutory interpretation to the international treaty context.[93] However, these suggestions essentially constitute arguments *de lege ferenda* concerning what the law may ideally encompass, rather than its present reality. As Schwarzenberger have implied regarding related topics,[94] such perspectives remain detached from the actual circumstances characterizing established international treaty interpretation.

If prescription of precise rule/method/guide for interpretation is lacking, does that necessarily imply an absence of constraints? While autointerpretation arises in international disputes, wildly divergent or illogical positions would not legally constitute disagreements amenable to adjudication. Even if interpretation is "an intellectual process that does not lend itself to a strict legal formulization,"[95] in any legal system, there seems to be a minimum standard asking this intellectual process to conform to common sense, reasonableness and logic. The constraints are not on the process of interpretation in terms of providing a precise rule/method/guide, as the process is indeed a "magic box" not subject to any legal formulization, but on the end

---

[90] Georg Schwarzenberger, "Myths and Realities of Treaty Interpretation: Articles 27–29 of the Vienna Draft Convention on the Law of Treaties," *Virginia Journal of International Law*, Vol. 9 (1968–1969), p. 7 (in such a situation, the first task would be to interpret the meaning of the term "special meaning" in the articles on interpretation… it can be done only by falling back on lex lata, that is, the rules of international customary law applicable to treaty interpretation).

[91] Articles 31 and 32 are binding treaty law for the parties to the Vienna Convention. They are at the same time codified customary international law. See *Territorial Dispute (Libya v. Chad), Judgment*, I.C.J. Reports 1994, p. 19, para. 41. For an overall discussion on the codification of pre-existing customary law in Articles 31–33, see Evan Criddle, "The Vienna Convention on the Law of Treaties in U.S. Treaty Interpretation," *Virginia Journal of International Law*, Vol. 44 (2003–2004), pp. 445–448.

[92] L. Oppenheim, *International Law* Vol. 1 (8th ed., edited by H. Lauterpacht, Longmans, 1955), p. 950 ("there are no precise rules of customary or conventional international law concerning the interpretation of treaties.").

[93] Justin Lowe, "What Would Grotius Do—Methods and Implications of Incorporating the Contract Law Doctrine of Illusory Promises into the Law of Treaty Interpretation," *Washington University Global Studies Law Review*, Vol. 6 (2007), p. 722 (Justin Lowe suggests incorporating the doctrine of illusory promise into the law of treaty interpretation. According to this theory, ambiguous treaty provisions could be invalidated under this doctrine, meaning treaties would be more likely to contain meaningful commitments). P. A Buttar, "Contextual Syntax of International Instruments Safeguarding against Nuclear Proliferation", *Australian Year Book of International Law*, Vol. 11 (1984–1987), pp. 148–150 (Buttar looked at doctrines other than Articles 31 and 32, such as rule of interpreting contract (contra proferentem rule) or the rule in interpreting statue (jusden generis)).

[94] Georg Schwarzenberger, *supra* note 90, p. 19.

[95] Edward Slavko Yambrusic, *supra* note 30, p. 249.

product of this magic process. If a resulting interpretation proves excessively strained or implausible, it risks compromising credibility in the interpretive undertaking as a whole.

Constraints on the end product stem from foundations of common sense, reasonableness and logic. Article 31 of the Vienna Convention on the Law of Treaties' stipulation of "good faith" reflects these constrains. While "good faith" conceptually arises from natural law and prohibits exploitation through an unintended literal reading that confers unjust benefit,[96] in application to treaty interpretation it associates closely with common sense and reasonableness.[97] Scholars occasionally describe its requirements and those of common sense as interchangeable.[98] "Good faith" is at times considered to entail maintaining consistency in interpretation.[99]

The International Court of Justice declined an inconsistent interpretive argument put forth by Greece in the *Aegean Sea Continental Shelf* case:

> If the Greek Government is correct, as it undoubtedly is, in assuming that the meaning of the generic term "rights" in Article 17 follows the evolution of the law, so as to be capable of embracing rights over the continental shelf, it is not clear why the similar term "territorial status" should not likewise be liable to evolve in meaning in accordance with "the development of international relations...."[100]

The requirement of logical coherence is implicit within the general rule of interpretation. As the International Law Commission astutely noted in commentary, when codifying disparate interpretive elements as a unified standard, the general rule's structure reflected "a consideration of logic, not any obligatory legal hierarchy."[101]

Common sense, reasonableness and logic were meant to constrain interpretive outcomes rather than the process itself. As the ILC commentary indicates:

> [W]hen a treaty is open to two interpretations one of which does and the other does not enable the treaty to have appropriate effects, good faith and the objects and purposes of the treaty demand that the former interpretation should be adopted.[102]

---

[96] Anthony D'Amato, "Good Faith," in *Max Planck Encyclopedia of Public International Law*(Elsevier Science Publishers and Max Planck Institute for Comparative Public Law and International Law, 1985), pp. 107–108.

[97] Georg Schwarzenberger, *supra* note 90, p. 10.

[98] Shabtai Rosenne, "Interpretation of Treaties in the Restatement and the International Law Commission's Draft Articles: A Comparison," *Columbia Journal of Transnational Law*, Vol. 5 (1966), p. 223 (noting that international jurisprudence contains many references to "good faith" in interpretation, or "reasonableness", which is much the same thing).

[99] Francis G. Jacobs, "Varieties of Approach to Treaty Interpretation: With Special Reference to the Draft Convention on the Law of Treaties before the Vienna Diplomatic Conference," *International and Comparative Law Quarterly*, Vol. 18 (1969), p. 333 (noting that good faith might be taken more narrowly, as precluding a State from exploiting an ambiguity in the text or a genuine misunderstanding between the parties. Alternatively, more broadly, a State might be precluded, in certain circumstances, from advancing an interpretation contrary to its own previous practice, or contrary to the shared expectations of the parties).

[100] *Aegean Sea Continental Shelf (Greece v. Turkey), Judgment*, I.C.J. Reports 1978, p. 33, para. 78.

[101] *Yearbook of the International Law Commission 1966 II*, p. 220.

[102] *Ibid.*, p. 219.

Reasonableness and common sense would permit recourse to supplementary means of interpretation if the application of Article 31 "leads to a result which is manifestly absurd or unreasonable."[103] Such standards likewise constrain Article 31's results without impeding the process itself. Specifically, where an outcome in applying Article 31 is deemed manifestly absurd or unreasonable, independent of scrutinizing the "magic box" workings, it may be deemed unacceptable and subject to reevaluation using supplementary means of treaty interpretation.

Interpretation, as an intricate intellectual process, necessitates flexibility for interpreters (States engaged in autointerpretation). Article 31 of the Vienna Convention on the Law of Treaties consolidates disparate interpretive considerations into a unified standard, acknowledging this facet.[104] Theoretically, this codification faces circularity critiques due to a paradox of *Quis custodiet ipsos custodes.* Practically, flexibility implies states may advance autointerpretations with initial reference to Article 31 elements, while an international court or tribunal may exercise discretion in settling interpretive disputes, depending on the States consenting to their jurisdictions.

Flexibility in interpretive methodology does not imply outcomes may contravene reasonableness, common sense and logic. Such results would prove untenable both in domestic and international legal systems. In international law, Article 31's core aim involves precluding spurious or fraudulent interpretations. To this end, a "good faith" requirement[105] implicitly demands adherence to reasonableness, common sense and logic. Such constraints feature not only judicially but also in autointerpretation, as states hold interests in reputations as good faith treaty adherents.[106]

In summary, the minimum constraint standard for treaty interpretation concerns not strict or perfect application of the general rule's methodology through a hypothetical hierarchy, but rather whether the result of the interpretation is reasonable, logical and in consistence with common sense—qualities demonstrating interpretation performed in "good faith" as Article 31 intends.

---

[103] Vienna Convention on the Law of Treaties, done at Vienna on May 23, 1969, entered into force on January 27, 1980, 1155 UNTS 331. Article 32.

[104] However, McDougal may have had a different view. See Myres S. McDougal, "The International Law Commission's Draft Articles upon Interpretation: Textuality Redivivus," *American Journal of International Law*, Vol. 61 (1967), p. 992 (noting that the great defect, and tragedy, in the International Law Commission's final recommendations about the interpretation of treaties is in their insistent emphasis upon an impossible, conformity-imposing textuality).

[105] *Ibid.*, p. 998, especially note 31.

[106] Ian Johnstone, "Treaty Interpretation: The Authority of Interpretive Communities," *Michigan Journal of International Law*, Vol. 12 (1990–1991), p. 390.

7.4 Conclusion

Article 31(3) (b) of the Vienna Convention on the Law of Treaties establishes a method for interpretation through subsequent practice by positioning consent or implied consent as the sole evaluative basis. However, investigations from *travaux préparatoires* of 1969 Vienna Convention on the Law of Treaties and international judicial practice confirm the distinction between modification and interpretation has been obscure. Additionally, the ILC commentary and international judicial practices highlight difficulties in ascertaining the subsequent practice relevant to "agreement of the Parties regarding its interpretation." Consequently, Article 31(3) (b) cannot be restricted solely to consent when evaluating subsequent practice's legal relevance to interpretation, given the law-making effect of the latter. Extra-consensual elements also factor into such determinations.

The Constructivist understanding of the current international system as an intersubjectively constructed society rather than a simple gathering of autonomous, self-interested, and rational states imbues consent with rich implication. Firstly, consent as a method in international law making does not lead to a Hobbesian understanding of international law that presents consent as the sole basis of obligation. Secondly, the constitutive or extraneous rules accompanying consent in international law making challenge traditional consent doctrine embracing formalistic, static treaty rules. Hence, assessment of subsequent practice in treaty application escapes binary legal–illegal evaluations relying on static treaty rules. As a corollary, subsequent practice in treaty application evades spurious claims of consent establishing authentic interpretations of such formalistic, static treaty rules.

Constructivists critiques at ontological and methodological levels aid clarifying approaches to better understand subsequent practice in treaty application. The Constructivists' ontological view of an intersubjectively constructed global society offers common ground across legal theories. As treaty interpretation through subsequent practice holds equivalent "law-making" effect, both consent and extraconsensual elements necessarily factor into what subsequent practice counts as "authentic interpretation," differing by legal theories. Whereas *pacta sunt servanda* implies static, regulatory treaty obligations, other legal theories suggest diversity of such validating extraneous rules—ranging from Hart's secondary rule to Frank's legitimacy concern and the New Haven School's emphasis on "human dignity," alongside Fuller's revived focus on "internal morality."[107]

[107] Jutta Brunnee and Stephen J. Toope, *super* note 79, pp. 19–74.

Chapter 8
Concluding Remarks

In contemporary treaty making, states frequently "agree to disagree" and deliberately introduce ambiguity into treaty provisions. The symptoms of fragmentation in treaty law are manifested through ambiguous treaty language and indeterminacy that facilitates such ambiguity. However, the root causes of fragmentation should not be solely attributed to language indeterminacy, but may also lie in the rapid changes in today's international relations landscape. The end of the Cold War, if not "the end of history," at least increased appeal of liberal democracy in world politics. Agenda setting now tends to privilege states with common interests of an emergent international "society." Meanwhile, it remains true that international relations fundamentally operate within a *laissez faire* system.

While emerging treaty regimes addressing areas like trade, the law of the sea, international protection of environment, and arms control were designed to consider common interests shared by humanity, they also necessitated balancing differing state interests in light of varying development levels. Today, it appears this balance has been judiciously maintained through what the present author calls "intentional ambiguity." That is, states leverage semantic indeterminacy to both maintain discrepancies while presenting a façade of consensus around agreed text. This allows states to demonstrate consideration of society-oriented common interests while still competing as autonomous actors conscious of their ultimate responsibility to ensure survival within a *laissez faire* international system.

In the nuclear nonproliferation regime, international coordination on controlling nuclear activities and technologies under the new regulatory institution (Nuclear Suppliers Group) has been supported by many NPT States Party. However, because some States Party imposed controls against others, a new line of "haves" and "have-nots" emerged beyond the discriminatory NPT through this subsequent practice. This situation created significant difficulty among States Party regarding interpretation of the "inalienable right" and related NPT articles. Regarding treaty interpretation, it would not be accurate to claim this type of subsequent practice alone establishes the

X. Zhang, *Law and Politics in Peaceful Use of Nuclear Energy*,
https://doi.org/10.1007/978-981-97-3813-7_8

agreement of the parties regarding the interpretation of the NPT given the lack of explicit response from regulated states.

In the past fifty years, whereas the threshold for accessing sensitive nuclear technology decreased and geopolitics underwent significant change, the common interest of the international community in countering nuclear proliferation—the core value of the NPT—has remained constant, garnering increasingly broad support. Clear evidence of general acceptance of this value is universal membership: today, 191 states belong to the NPT, a number no less impressive than the United Nations' 193 members. Moreover, the decision at the 1995 NPT Review Conference to extend the treaty indefinitely signaled resolute international societal backing for the NPT.

States' sovereign right (inalienable right) to peaceful use of nuclear energy, and public interest in nonproliferation, may warrant reconsideration and reconstruction in light of technological and political developments. An authoritative interpretation of the "inalienable right" referenced in Article IV of the NPT could help inform such efforts. However, given the lack of dispute settlement mechanism within that treaty, it is unlikely that states in disagreement over new control measures could obtain definitive legal clarity on the issue from an international judicial body. The 1995 NPT Review and Extension Conference presented an important opportunity for States Party to reach agreement within the Decisions of the Conference on clarifying the scope of "inalienable right" referenced in Article IV. While a more expansive interpretation of that right to peaceful use was speculated as part of negotiations over indefinite extension of the NPT, the actual decision regarding Article IV ultimately reflected political compromise rather than legal resolution. That failure of past NPT Review Conferences to achieve consensus on interpreting this right regarding peaceful use of nuclear energy is unfortunate. Records of previous Review Conferences clearly illustrate the interplay between law and politics in the field of nuclear nonproliferation as a pivotal issue therein.

This study of the interplay between law and politics in the realm of peaceful use of nuclear energy originated from observations of the debate surrounding multilateral nuclear export controls. Interpretation of "inalienable right" and associated NPT provisions were highly salient issues therein. A substantial body of literature argued for or against proposed nuclear export control measures on the basis of legal–illegal determinations derived from respective interpretations of "inalienable right." Notably, each position found support within ambiguous text of the treaty. Discussion of the measures' legality ultimately concluded in an impasse of "autointerpretation," with opposing legal-illegal judgments on multilateral export controls binding none and convincing few.

In the debate, the "inalienable right" and associated provisions of the NPT were viewed as a set of static, regulative rules. However, this perspective overlooks the intentionally designed dynamic obligations within these provisions, a fact verifiable through revisiting the NPT negotiations. The NPT also establishes a Review Conference mechanism allowing periodic review of treaty implementation. Through this process, States Party presume their willingness to consensually refine treaty relations over time.

This study argues that uncertainty surrounding nuclear technology and evolving geopolitical contexts informed provisions for dynamic treaty obligations within certain NPT articles. An examination of pre-NPT U.S. nuclear controls demonstrates uncertainties stemming from limited technological knowledge and application. This led the U.S. to reconsider narrowly construing national interests in security terms alone, broadening its perspective to include potential economic benefits from civilian nuclear commerce. Technological uncertainty primarily shaped the NPT's dynamic design. In addition, the "logic of appropriateness" helps explain why some countries during negotiations embrace dynamic treaty obligations, seeking to avoid disruption from a "normative shift" concerning nonproliferation.

This study argues that states intentionally crafted dynamic obligations within NPT provisions during treaty-making. Evidence from an investigation of the negotiating process and the *travaux préparatoires* of the NPT strongly support this view. The investigation examined the drafting of the "inalienable right" and "the right to participate" clauses in Article IV, as well as the contextual reading of Article II. It indicates powerful states in the drafting process, such as the United States, advocated ambiguity regarding the "inalienable right," despite other countries' efforts for clarification; the ambiguous text survived adoption. Based on these findings, the study questions the overstated presumption of the traditional consent doctrine that states only opt for unambiguous, determinant language in treaty-making. The sources of imprecision and contradiction in the text of the relevant NPT articles were uncertainty over nuclear technology as well as dynamic national interests shaped by evolving normative circumstances.

Treaty interpretation constitutes a central issue. Article 31 of the Vienna Convention on the Laws of Treaties codifies a general rule favoring a textual–contextual approach, emphasizing the text as a starting point while allowing for other extra-textual factors having logical connections in the interpretive process. However, criticism arises regarding this "general rule of treaty interpretation," as the "ending point" of any interpretation remains undefined, and interpreting the general rule itself requires further interpretation. In practice, judicial bodies often apply interpretive logic contextually, both regionally and culturally, diminishing reliance on codified rules for any given interpretation.

This study questions the usefulness of the general rule of interpretation codified in the Vienna Convention on the Law of Treaties and proposes an interdisciplinary lens to better understand dynamic treaty obligations in the nuclear nonproliferation regime. For many international lawyers, treaty interpretation, or more precisely applying the general rule of treaty interpretation, appears mythic. However, the present author argues this myth arises from a rule-based legal perspective grounded in limited assumptions. Instead, treaty interpretation is viewed not as an unsolvable myth but rather an intricate puzzle amenable to broader examination incorporating perspectives from the study of the rules and norms in international relations.

This study outlines Constructivists' contributions to addressing treaty interpretation. Constructivists accord international norms and institutions equal ontological standing with material existence, viewing them as constituting the intersubjective world. Ontologically, Constructivists see treaty rules as evolving social structures rather than solely static regulations. Methodologically, Constructivists reject positivist behavioral and inductive legal approaches that distort intersubjective construction. Linguistically, Constructivists recognize language's indeterminate nature. All of them offer insight into the nature of international legal obligations. Language challenges rule-based legal thinking and the associated text–context approach to treaty interpretation in certain respects. For instance, interpreting the interplay between subsequent practice and dynamic treaty obligations necessitates consideration of some extraconsensual rules/norms, rejecting the traditional view of consent as the sole foundation of international law and of national interests as fixedly materialistic and stable. Overall, Constructivism provides a theoretical foundation for those international lawyers who view the legal system as an ongoing, never-finished process rather than one composed soley static, regulatory rules.

Now, how shall we understand subsequent practice in applying dynamic treaty obligations generally and specifically within the NPT? From the traditional positivist view, unless subsequent practice in the application of the treaty establishes the Parties' agreement, it cannot be regarded as authentic interpretation of such obligations. In such a case, subsequent practice may be left for autointerpretation by the States Party. Dynamic treaty obligations could also potentially undergo judicial interpretation. However, given the circumstances, this resolution likely would have proven impractical.

This study argues that multilateral nuclear export controls cannot be considered solely within the framework of legal–illegal judgments based on textual–contextual interpretation of relevant NPT articles. Interpreting the dynamic "inalienable right" calls into question not just the viability of judgments derived from a traditional "general rule of treaty interpretation," but also suggests the contribution of multilateral nuclear controls to the development of dynamic obligations regarding this right. Multilateral nuclear export controls are also understood to inform evolving obligations connected to the "inalienable right." During the process, Fuller's internal morality regarding promulgation was seen as important to narrowing gaps between supplier and recipient countries. It required improving transparency of export controls and establishing a framework for dialog and cooperation on multilateral measures among all interested NPT States Party. This need signaled movement toward a new consensus on "interpreting" the evolving nuclear nonproliferation regime, which emerged from disagreement over enhanced discriminatory control regimes.

Two potential approaches could help resolve issues of "intentional ambiguity." At the micro-level, given states further define ambiguities, treaty regimes could establish an "authoritative interpretation" process respecting the crucial role of state consent in international law and international relations.[1] For multilateral treaties pursuing "common interests," some scholars propose a model of "multilateral mechanism" used in environmental agreements where Meeting/Conference of Parties (MOP/COP) make decisions based not just on individual state interests but a shared legal

[1] Eric J. Pan, "Authoritative Interpretation of Agreements: Developing More Responsive International Administrative Regimes," *Harvard International Law Journal*, Vol. 38 (1997), p. 530.

framework governing the treaty's formation.[2] At the macro-level, without universal third-party oversight in the current decentralized system, states more often engage in autointerpretations of treaties. A minimum standard holding reasonableness, logic and common sense is needed in evaluating various "autointerpretations." Such constraints help ensure states abide by requirements to act in "good faith," as defined in Article 31 of the Vienna Convention on the Law of Treaties.

Certain United States autointerpretations in the field of nuclear technology and activity have faced question, such as its "selective policy" approach. This diverged from earlier positions adopted by the U.S. and appears inconsistent with the non-discriminatory logic underpinning the NPT, which distinguishes solely the nuclear-weapon states and the non-nuclear-weapon states, not among the latter regardless of labeling, such as "rogue states" or "evil states." Such interpretations seem to lack good faith and risk undermining perceived legitimacy of the international order through inviting legitimate objections.[3]

---

[2] Atsuko Kanehara, "Some Considerations Regarding Methods of International Regulation in Global Issues: Sovereignty and Common Interests," *Studies in Transnational Legal Policy,* Vol. 29 (1997), p. 112.

[3] Richard Falk, "The Illegitimacy of the Non-Proliferation Regime," *Brown Journal of World Affairs,* Vol. 4 (1997), p. 74, p. 81.

Annex: Treaty on the Non-proliferation of Nuclear Weapons (1968)

The States concluding this Treaty, hereinafter referred to as the "Parties to the Treaty".[1]

Considering the devastation that would be visited upon all mankind by a nuclear war and the consequent need to make every effort to avert the danger of such a war and to take measures to safeguard the security of peoples.

Believing that the proliferation of nuclear weapons would seriously enhance the danger of nuclear war.

In conformity with resolutions of the United Nations General Assembly calling for the conclusion of an agreement on the prevention of wider dissemination of nuclear weapons.

Undertaking to co-operate in facilitating the application of International Atomic Energy Agency safeguards on peaceful nuclear activities.

Expressing their support for research, development and other efforts to further the application, within the framework of the International Atomic Energy Agency safeguards system, of the principle of safeguarding effectively the flow of source and special fissionable materials by use of instruments and other techniques at certain strategic points.

Affirming the principle that the benefits of peaceful applications of nuclear technology, including any technological by-products which may be derived by nuclear-weapon States from the development of nuclear explosive devices, should be available for peaceful purposes to all Parties to the Treaty, whether nuclear-weapon or non-nuclear-weapon States.

Convinced that, in furtherance of this principle, all Parties to the Treaty are entitled to participate in the fullest possible exchange of scientific information for, and to contribute alone or in co-operation with other States to, the further development of the applications of atomic energy for peaceful purposes.

[1] Treaty on the Nonproliferation of Nuclear Weapons (NPT), opened for signature July 1, 1968, entered into force March 5, 1970, extended indefinitely in the 1995 NPT Review and Extension Conference), 729 UNTS 161.

X. Zhang, *Law and Politics in Peaceful Use of Nuclear Energy*,
https://doi.org/10.1007/978-981-97-3813-7

Declaring their intention to achieve at the earliest possible date the cessation of the nuclear arms race and to undertake effective measures in the direction of nuclear disarmament.

Urging the co-operation of all States in the attainment of this objective.

Recalling the determination expressed by the Parties to the 1963 Treaty banning nuclear weapon tests in the atmosphere, in outer space and under water in its Preamble to seek to achieve the discontinuance of all test explosions of nuclear weapons for all time and to continue negotiations to this end.

Desiring to further the easing of international tension and the strengthening of trust between States in order to facilitate the cessation of the manufacture of nuclear weapons, the liquidation of all their existing stockpiles, and the elimination from national arsenals of nuclear weapons and the means of their delivery pursuant to a Treaty on general and complete disarmament under strict and effective international control.

Recalling that, in accordance with the Charter of the United Nations, States must refrain in their international relations from the threat or use of force against the territorial integrity or political independence of any State, or in any other manner inconsistent with the Purposes of the United Nations, and that the establishment and maintenance of international peace and security are to be promoted with the least diversion for armaments of the world's human and economic resources.

Have agreed as follows:

Article I

Each nuclear-weapon State Party to the Treaty undertakes not to transfer to any recipient whatsoever nuclear weapons or other nuclear explosive devices or control over such weapons or explosive devices directly, or indirectly; and not in any way to assist, encourage, or induce any non-nuclear-weapon State to manufacture or otherwise acquire nuclear weapons or other nuclear explosive devices, or control over such weapons or explosive devices.

Article II

Each non-nuclear-weapon State Party to the Treaty undertakes not to receive the transfer from any transferor whatsoever of nuclear weapons or other nuclear explosive devices or of control over such weapons or explosive devices directly, or indirectly; not to manufacture or otherwise acquire nuclear weapons or other nuclear explosive devices; and not to seek or receive any assistance in the manufacture of nuclear weapons or other nuclear explosive devices.

Article III

1. Each non-nuclear-weapon State Party to the Treaty undertakes to accept safeguards, as set forth in an agreement to be negotiated and concluded with the International Atomic Energy Agency in accordance with the Statute of the International Atomic Energy Agency and the Agency's safeguards system, for the exclusive purpose of verification of the fulfilment of its obligations assumed under this Treaty with a view to preventing diversion of nuclear energy from

peaceful uses to nuclear weapons or other nuclear explosive devices. Procedures for the safeguards required by this Article shall be followed with respect to source or special fissionable material whether it is being produced, processed or used in any principal nuclear facility or is outside any such facility. The safeguards required by this Article shall be applied on all source or special fissionable material in all peaceful nuclear activities within the territory of such State, under its jurisdiction, or carried out under its control anywhere.

2. Each State Party to the Treaty undertakes not to provide: (a) source or special fissionable material, or (b) equipment or material especially designed or prepared for the processing, use or production of special fissionable material, to any non-nuclear-weapon State for peaceful purposes, unless the source or special fissionable material shall be subject to the safeguards required by this Article.
3. The safeguards required by this Article shall be implemented in a manner designed to comply with Article IV of this Treaty, and to avoid hampering the economic or technological development of the Parties or international co-operation in the field of peaceful nuclear activities, including the international exchange of nuclear material and equipment for the processing, use or production of nuclear material for peaceful purposes in accordance with the provisions of this Article and the principle of safeguarding set forth in the Preamble of the Treaty.
4. Non-nuclear-weapon States Party to the Treaty shall conclude agreements with the International Atomic Energy Agency to meet the requirements of this Article either individually or together with other States in accordance with the Statute of the International Atomic Energy Agency. Negotiation of such agreements shall commence within 180 days from the original entry into force of this Treaty. For States depositing their instruments of ratification or accession after the 180-day period, negotiation of such agreements shall commence not later than the date of such deposit. Such agreements shall enter into force not later than eighteen months after the date of initiation of negotiations.

Article IV

1. Nothing in this Treaty shall be interpreted as affecting the inalienable right of all the Parties to the Treaty to develop research, production and use of nuclear energy for peaceful purposes without discrimination and in conformity with Articles I and II of this Treaty.
2. All the Parties to the Treaty undertake to facilitate, and have the right to participate in, the fullest possible exchange of equipment, materials and scientific and technological information for the peaceful uses of nuclear energy. Parties to the Treaty in a position to do so shall also co-operate in contributing alone or together with other States or international organizations to the further development of the applications of nuclear energy for peaceful purposes, especially in the territories of non-nuclear-weapon States Party to the Treaty, with due consideration for the needs of the developing areas of the world.

Article V

Each Party to the Treaty undertakes to take appropriate measures to ensure that, in accordance with this Treaty, under appropriate international observation and through appropriate international procedures, potential benefits from any peaceful applications of nuclear explosions will be made available to non-nuclear-weapon States Party to the Treaty on a non-discriminatory basis and that the charge to such Parties for the explosive devices used will be as low as possible and exclude any charge for research and development. Non-nuclear-weapon States Party to the Treaty shall be able to obtain such benefits, pursuant to a special international agreement or agreements, through an appropriate international body with adequate representation of non-nuclear-weapon States. Negotiations on this subject shall commence as soon as possible after the Treaty enters into force. Non-nuclear-weapon States Party to the Treaty so desiring may also obtain such benefits pursuant to bilateral agreements.

Article VI

Each of the Parties to the Treaty undertakes to pursue negotiations in good faith on effective measures relating to cessation of the nuclear arms race at an early date and to nuclear disarmament, and on a treaty on general and complete disarmament under strict and effective international control.

Article VII

Nothing in this Treaty affects the right of any group of States to conclude regional treaties in order to assure the total absence of nuclear weapons in their respective territories.

Article VIII

1. Any Party to the Treaty may propose amendments to this Treaty. The text of any proposed amendment shall be submitted to the Depositary Governments which shall circulate it to all Parties to the Treaty. Thereupon, if requested to do so by one-third or more of the Parties to the Treaty, the Depositary Governments shall convene a conference, to which they shall invite all the Parties to the Treaty, to consider such an amendment.
2. Any amendment to this Treaty must be approved by a majority of the votes of all the Parties to the Treaty, including the votes of all nuclear-weapon States Party to the Treaty and all other Parties which, on the date the amendment is circulated, are members of the Board of Governors of the International Atomic Energy Agency. The amendment shall enter into force for each Party that deposits its instrument of ratification of the amendment upon the deposit of such instruments of ratification by a majority of all the Parties, including the instruments of ratification of all nuclear-weapon States Party to the Treaty and all other Parties which, on the date the amendment is circulated, are members of the Board of Governors of the International Atomic Energy Agency. Thereafter, it shall enter into force for any other Party upon the deposit of its instrument of ratification of the amendment.

3. Five years after the entry into force of this Treaty, a conference of Parties to the Treaty shall be held in Geneva, Switzerland, in order to review the operation of this Treaty with a view to assuring that the purposes of the Preamble and the provisions of the Treaty are being realised. At intervals of five years thereafter, a majority of the Parties to the Treaty may obtain, by submitting a proposal to this effect to the Depositary Governments, the convening of further conferences with the same objective of reviewing the operation of the Treaty.

Article IX

1. This Treaty shall be open to all States for signature. Any State which does not sign the Treaty before its entry into force in accordance with paragraph 3 of this Article may accede to it at any time.
2. This Treaty shall be subject to ratification by signatory States. Instruments of ratification and instruments of accession shall be deposited with the Governments of the United Kingdom of Great Britain and Northern Ireland, the Union of Soviet Socialist Republics and the United States of America, which are hereby designated the Depositary Governments.
3. This Treaty shall enter into force after its ratification by the States, the Governments of which are designated Depositaries of the Treaty, and forty other States signatory to this Treaty and the deposit of their instruments of ratification. For the purposes of this Treaty, a nuclear-weapon State is one which has manufactured and exploded a nuclear weapon or other nuclear explosive device prior to 1 January, 1967.
4. For States whose instruments of ratification or accession are deposited subsequent to the entry into force of this Treaty, it shall enter into force on the date of the deposit of their instruments of ratification or accession.
5. The Depositary Governments shall promptly inform all signatory and acceding States of the date of each signature, the date of deposit of each instrument of ratification or of accession, the date of the entry into force of this Treaty, and the date of receipt of any requests for convening a conference or other notices.
6. This Treaty shall be registered by the Depositary Governments pursuant to Article 102 of the Charter of the United Nations.

Article X

1. Each Party shall in exercising its national sovereignty have the right to withdraw from the Treaty if it decides that extraordinary events, related to the subject matter of this Treaty, have jeopardized the supreme interests of its country. It shall give notice of such withdrawal to all other Parties to the Treaty and to the United Nations Security Council three months in advance. Such notice shall include a statement of the extraordinary events it regards as having jeopardized its supreme interests.
2. Twenty-five years after the entry into force of the Treaty, a conference shall be convened to decide whether the Treaty shall continue in force indefinitely, or shall be extended for an additional fixed period or periods. This decision shall be taken by a majority of the Parties to the Treaty.

Article XI

This Treaty, the English, Russian, French, Spanish and Chinese texts of which are equally authentic, shall be deposited in the archives of the Depositary Governments. Duly certified copies of this Treaty shall be transmitted by the Depositary Governments to the Governments of the signatory and acceding States.

IN WITNESS WHEREOF the undersigned, duly authorised, have signed this Treaty.

DONE in triplicate, at the cities of London, Moscow and Washington, the first day of July, one thousand nine hundred and sixty-eight.

Index

X. Zhang, *Law and Politics in Peaceful Use of Nuclear Energy*,
https://doi.org/10.1007/978-981-97-3813-7